INTRODUCING
ISSUES WITH
OPPOSING
VIEWPOINTS®

Homosexuality

Other books in the Introducing Issues
with Opposing Viewpoints series:

AIDS
Civil Liberties
Cloning
The Death Penalty
Gangs
Gay Marriage
Genetic Engineering
Smoking
Terrorism

INTRODUCING
ISSUES WITH
OPPOSING
VIEWPOINTS®

Homosexuality

Emma Bernay, *Book Editor*

Christina Nasso, *Publisher*
Elizabeth Des Chenes, *Managing Editor*

GREENHAVEN PRESS
A part of Gale, Cengage Learning

GALE
CENGAGE Learning·

Detroit • New York • San Francisco • New Haven, Conn • Waterville, Maine • London

For more information, contact
Greenhaven Press
27500 Drake Rd.
Farmington Hills, MI 48331-3535
Or you can visit our Internet site at gale.cengage.com

LIBRARY OF CONGRESS CATALOGING-IN-PUBLICATION DATA

Homosexuality / Emma Bernay, book editor.
   p. cm. — (Introducing issues with opposing viewpoints)
   Includes bibliographical references and index.
   ISBN-13: 978-0-7377-3852-0 (hardcover)
   1. Homosexuality—United States.   2. Gays—United States.   3. Gay rights—
United States.   4. Same-sex marriage—United States.   I. Bernay, Emma.
   HQ76.3.U5H6444 2007
   306.76′60973—dc22
                                                              2007030379

ISBN-10: 0-7377-3852-9 (hardcover)

Printed in the United States of America
  3 4 5 6 7 12 11 10 09 08

Contents

Chapter 3: Should Gay People Be Permitted to Marry?

Indulging in a wide spectrum of ideas, beliefs, and perspectives is a critical cornerstone of democracy. After all, it is often debates over differences of opinion, such as whether to legalize abortion, how to treat prisoners, or when to enact the death penalty that shape our society and drive it forward. Such diversity of thought is frequently regarded as the hallmark of a healthy and civilized culture. As the Reverend Clifford Schutjer of the First Congregational Church in Mansfield, Ohio, declared in a 2001 sermon, "Surrounding oneself with only like-minded people, restricting what we listen to or read only to what we find agreeable is irresponsible. Refusing to entertain doubts once we make up our minds is a subtle but deadly form of arrogance." With this advice in mind, Introducing Issues with Opposing Viewpoints books aim to open readers' minds to the critically divergent views that comprise our world's most important debates.

Introducing Issues with Opposing Viewpoints simplifies for students the enormous and often overwhelming mass of material now available via print and electronic media. Collected in every volume is an array of opinions that capture the essence of a particular controversy or topic. Introducing Issues with Opposing Viewpoints books embody the spirit of nineteenth-century journalist Charles A. Dana's axiom: "Fight for your opinions, but do not believe that they contain the whole truth, or the only truth." Absorbing such contrasting opinions teaches students to analyze the strength of an argument and compare it to its opposition. From this process readers can inform and strengthen their own opinions, or be exposed to new information that will change their minds. Introducing Issues with Opposing Viewpoints is a mosaic of different voices. The authors are statesmen, pundits, academics, journalists, corporations, and ordinary people who have felt compelled to share their experiences and ideas in a public forum. Their words have been collected from newspapers, journals, books, speeches, interviews, and the Internet, the fastest growing body of opinionated material in the world.

Introducing Issues with Opposing Viewpoints shares many of the well-known features of its critically acclaimed parent series, Opposing Viewpoints. The articles are presented in a pro/con format, allowing readers to absorb divergent perspectives side by side. Active reading questions preface each viewpoint, requiring the student to approach the material thoughtfully and carefully. Useful charts, graphs, and cartoons supplement each article. A thorough introduction provides readers with crucial background on an issue. An annotated bibliography points the reader toward articles, books, and Web sites that contain additional information on the topic. An appendix of organizations to contact contains a wide variety of charities, nonprofit organizations, political groups, and private enterprises that each hold a position on the issue at hand. Finally, a comprehensive index allows readers to locate content quickly and efficiently.

Introducing Issues with Opposing Viewpoints is also significantly different from Opposing Viewpoints. As the series title implies, its presentation will help introduce students to the concept of opposing viewpoints, and learn to use this material to aid in critical writing and debate. The series' four-color, accessible format makes the books attractive and inviting to readers of all levels. In addition, each viewpoint has been carefully edited to maximize a reader's understanding of the content. Short but thorough viewpoints capture the essence of an argument. A substantial, thought-provoking essay question placed at the end of each viewpoint asks the student to further investigate the issues raised in the viewpoint, compare and contrast two authors' arguments, or consider how one might go about forming an opinion on the topic at hand. Each viewpoint contains sidebars that include at-a-glance information and handy statistics. A Facts About section located in the back of the book further supplies students with relevant facts and figures.

Following in the tradition of the Opposing Viewpoints series, Greenhaven Press continues to provide readers with invaluable exposure to the controversial issues that shape our world. As John Stuart Mill once wrote: "The only way in which a human being can make some approach to knowing the whole of a subject is by hearing what can be said about it by persons of every variety of opinion and studying all modes in which it can be looked at by every character of mind. No wise man ever acquired his wisdom in any mode but this." It is to this principle that Introducing Issues with Opposing Viewpoints books are dedicated.

Introduction

"One of the most persistent debates surrounding homosexuality regards whether gays are 'born that way' or whether homosexuality is a 'chosen lifestyle.'"

—John Corvino, author and lecturer in philosophy, Wayne State University

Americans and other global citizens have long struggled with the issue of homosexuality. Records of same-sex relationships have been found in nearly every culture throughout history, but gay people have experienced varying degrees of acceptance at different times. In the days of ancient Greece, for instance, homosexual behavior was not only tolerated, it was considered as natural as heterosexual behavior. In some Middle Eastern countries today, the opposite is true: Homosexual expression is forbidden and severely punished by law. For American society in the twenty-first century, the issue is not so clear. On the one hand, gay people are not punished for living together or showing affection in public. Furthermore, in 2003, the Supreme Court struck down the country's remaining antihomosexuality laws in its decision in *Lawrence v. Texas*. Yet many social issues organizations and religious groups still believe that same-sex relationships are immoral and wrong. Some believe that homosexuals are even dangerous to children.

The discussion surrounding homosexuality has at its heart a main question: How is homosexuality categorized? Some groups, including gay advocacy organizations such as the Human Rights Campaign and the Parents and Friends of Lesbians and Gays (PFLAG), believe that homosexuality is akin to race, gender, and religion: a minority group whose members are a legitimate part of society and should be protected as such. Others, including such conservative groups as Concerned Women for America and Focus on the Family, believe that homosexuality is a conscious, deviant lifestyle choice—similar, perhaps, to polygamy or bestiality—that should not necessarily be protected by civil rights laws.

Depending on which category homosexuality is placed into, gay people are subject to different laws and protections. If homosexuality is equated the same status as race or gender, then gay people would have the right to marry each other, adopt children, hold any job, and join the military without restrictions. They would also be protected by equal opportunity laws, enabling them to sue if they experience discrimination because of their sexual orientation. When homosexuality is categorized as a deviant lifestyle, however, gay people are subject to many restrictions. Their behavior and living situations would be considered outside of the acceptable societal norm. They would not be protected under civil rights laws.

Many believe that the question "How should homosexuality be categorized?" can be answered with another question: Are people born gay? If homosexuality is considered genetic, it would be viewed as a natural state of being, like being black or being Jewish. This is because American society does not permit discrimination against people on the basis of their human conditions. However, if it is believed that homosexuality is a conscious choice, different laws would apply. For the most part, people tend to divide themselves into two distinct groups depending on their beliefs about the genetic basis of homosexuality.

The Human Rights Campaign, the Gay and Lesbian Alliance Against Defamation, and other social justice groups have long worked to promote gay civil rights. Gays cannot help how they are, nor should they, these organizations believe. Same-sex relationships are neither dangerous nor immoral, they state, and therefore gays should not be penalized for how they live their lives. Steve Swayne, a gay writer and professor, wrote in the *Vermont/New Hampshire Valley News*, "We are reaching a showdown in our culture war about where gay men and lesbians fit in American life. Many citizens believe that gays are morally degenerate. . . . Others believe that in a nation founded on the principle of liberty and justice for all, gay Americans are entitled to the same rights as every other American."[1]

Other socially conservative organizations and some religious groups shun the idea that the gay lifestyle is legitimate. Some view homosexuality as immoral. Many of these groups use a religious argument to

[1]Steve Swayne, "The Case for Federal Civil Unions," *Vermont/New Hampshire Valley News*, February 28, 2004.

support their views. For instance, Don Wildmon, founder of the conservative Christian group the American Family Association, discusses one aspect of this, gay marriage, in an article in the *American Family Association Journal.* "Homosexual marriage goes against the 'laws of nature and nature's God,'" he writes. "Every time you go against the law you pay. The problem is that by the time we admit that we have gone against the 'laws of nature and nature's God,' the damage has already been done."[2] Homosexuality is unnatural, according to this point of view. Those who choose this deviant behavior cannot ask that they be protected by law.

Though the gay rights movement in America is almost forty years old, the debate over homosexuality is far from reaching resolution. Gay marriage, for instance, has been an issue of particular concern in the twenty-first century. Many gay people and their supporters have advocated for their right to legally marry their partners. In 2004, the state of Massachusetts made history when it legitimized same-sex marriage—the only state to do so as of the time of this writing. In contrast, several states, including Arkansas, Georgia, and Kentucky, have passed laws specifically banning gay marriage. In 2004, President George W. Bush proposed an amendment to the U.S. Constitution that would prohibit same-sex marriages. However, the amendment failed to pass Congress in 2006. Other issues, such as gays in the military and health-care benefits for partners of gay people, have been equally as contentious.

Many have pushed strongly for full acceptance of gays into mainstream American society. Others have resisted this push just as vehemently. Both sides believe that they are working to uphold the fundamental norms of morality and justice. *Introducing Issues with Opposing Viewpoints: Homosexuality* discusses various aspects of this important debate in order to offer insight and understanding.

[2] Don Wildmon, "The Consequences of Same-Sex 'Marriage' Will Be Far Reaching," *American Family Association Journal,* April 2004.

Chapter 1

Is Homosexuality a Moral Issue?

Same-sex marriage supporters fight to have homosexuality seen as more than just a moral issue.

Homosexuality Is Immoral

Peter Sprigg

> *"I do not believe that engaging in behavior that is unnatural [and] immoral . . . is the best thing for people with same-sex attractions."*

In the following viewpoint, author Peter Sprigg argues that homosexuality is an unnatural, immoral state of being that threatens the fabric of society: family and children. Homosexuals are a dangerous influence on the world, Sprigg writes. They have a specific agenda that they are working to advance. This agenda attempts to give homosexuals special rights, Sprigg argues, over and above those who are living a moral life. Peter Sprigg is vice president for policy at the Family Research Council, a conservative social policy group. This viewpoint is excerpted from a speech Sprigg gave at the World Congress of Families in Mexico City.

AS YOU READ, CONSIDER THE FOLLOWING QUESTIONS:

1. According to the author, what is the definition of an ideal family?
2. What answer does the author provide for the question "Why is it that one of these threats—homosexuality—gets so much attention?
3. Name the fifth element in the homosexual agenda, according to the viewpoint.

Peter Sprigg, "Homosexuality: The Threat to the Family and the Attack on Marriage," Speech, World Congress of Families III, Mexico City, Mexico, March 29, 2004.

After individual human life itself, nothing is more precious or more essential to the survival and the success of human society than the family. The family is more important than the United Nations, more important than our individual countries, and more important than our cities, towns, or villages. The family is more important than our schools, corporations, or our civic organizations.

The family is more important than all of these things, because human civilization is built from the bottom up, not the top down. The first brick of the foundation is individual human life, and the second brick is the family. This raises crucial questions: What is a family? What makes a family?

Some people answer that question by saying, "Love makes a family." That sounds nice, but while love is, as the saying goes, "a many-splendored thing," love alone is not enough to make a family. In truth, what makes a family is one man and one woman united in marriage for a lifetime, and the children born from that union.

Not All Families Are Ideal

Not every family lives up to that ideal. Some people become single parents through no fault of their own, because of death or abandonment. Some loving couples adopt children in order to create a new family structure that reproduces as closely as possible the circumstances of a natural family. But it is important for society to continue to uphold the traditional family structure as the ideal family. It is important to uphold that ideal because it is the family structure most consistent with what the American Declaration of Independence refers to as "the laws of nature and of nature's God."

However, even if someone doesn't believe in natural law, or even in God, there is still a good reason to uphold the ideal of the traditional family.

The reason the married, one-man, one-woman natural family is the ideal family is that we know that both the spouses and the children in such families have a better chance in life. Such children, for instance, do better academically, financially, emotionally, and behaviorally. They have better health, and they delay sexual activity longer. The evidence for this in the social science literature is overwhelming.

It is because the family is so crucial to society that we call ourselves "pro-family." We want to do everything we can to support, encourage,

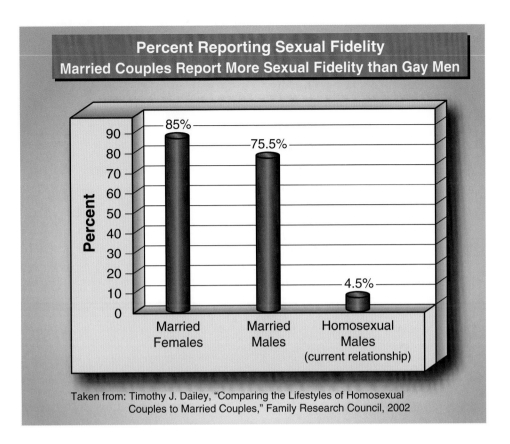

Percent Reporting Sexual Fidelity

Married Couples Report More Sexual Fidelity than Gay Men

Taken from: Timothy J. Dailey, "Comparing the Lifestyles of Homosexual Couples to Married Couples," Family Research Council, 2002

assist, maintain, and promote traditional families and do everything we can to maintain that ideal of the married one-man, one-woman natural family.

Homosexuality Undermines the Family

However, in order to defend what we are for—the family—we often must define what we are against. We are against anything that threatens the traditional family or undermines that ideal. That means that we are against parents snuffing out the lives of their own unborn children through abortion. It means that we are against drug and alcohol abuse, domestic violence, and child abuse. It means that we are against illegitimacy, abandonment, and divorce. And it means that we are against any sexual behavior that would undermine the uniqueness of the faithful, lifelong marriage bond between a husband and wife. We are against premarital sex, pornography, adultery, and prostitution. And yes, we are also against the practice of homosexuality.

Many people with strong religious beliefs view homosexuality as an act against God.

Now, you may ask, if we are for something so simple and profound as family, and against so many things that threaten it, why is it that one of these threats—homosexuality—gets so much attention? It's not because homosexuality is a greater sin than any other. It's not because we want to deprive homosexuals of their fundamental human rights. It's not because we are afraid to be near homosexuals, and it's not because we hate homosexuals. On the contrary, I desire the very best for them. And desiring the best for someone, and acting to bring that about, is the essence of love. However, I do not believe that engaging in behavior that is unnatural, immoral, and dangerous both to public health and to their own health is the best thing for people with same-sex attractions.

Homosexuals Have an Agenda

And so, as one part of our broad-based efforts to support the traditional family, we oppose what is sometimes called "the gay agenda." It is an agenda that demands the full acceptance of the practice of homosexuality—morally, socially, legally, religiously, politically, and financially. Indeed, it calls for not only acceptance, but affirmation and celebration of this behavior as normal. It even demands that homosexuality be seen as desirable for those who desire it. This is "the gay agenda"—and we are against it.

This agenda has already made remarkable progress. Homosexual activists knew that their behavior would never be accepted as

"normal" if doctors considered it a form of mental illness. Therefore, in 1973 they forced a resolution through the American Psychiatric Association to remove homosexuality from the Diagnostic and Statistical Manual of Mental Disorders. It is important for everyone to realize that the 1973 decision was *not* the result of new clinical research or scientific evidence. It was, rather, a *political* decision made in response to a vicious campaign of harassment and intimidation by homosexual activists. . . .

Homosexuals Want Special Rights

A second element in the agenda is to persuade people that those who engage in homosexual behavior are "born that way." If people are "born gay," it makes it more difficult to argue that a homosexual orientation is abnormal, or that homosexual behavior is immoral. It is astonishing how pervasive this concept has become—especially in light of the fact that there is *no* convincing scientific evidence that homosexuality is determined by either genetics or biology. Only a tiny handful of studies have ever been put forward to make such a claim. Unfortunately, the scientific critiques that discredited those studies have never quite caught up to the original media hype.

A third element of the homosexual agenda is to get "sexual orientation" added to the categories of protection under anti-discrimination codes in private organizations and under civil rights laws in the public sector. In fact, homosexuals should and already do have all of the same rights under the law as any other citizen, such as the right to vote, the right of free speech, and the right to trial by jury. Those rights are truly "civil" or political in nature, and the exercise of them does nothing to infringe on anyone else's freedom. . . .

A fourth element of the agenda is to win the enactment of "hate crime" laws that provide severe punishment of crimes motivated by "bias" against homosexuals. All of us in the pro-family movement are opposed to violent crimes, against homosexuals or anyone else. Hate crime laws, though, set a dangerous precedent of punishing people specifically for their opinions. In addition, under some such laws a person can be punished simply for intimidation—which could include just verbally expressing disapproval of homosexuality. One example comes from England, where 69-year-old Harry Hammond held a sign that said, "Stop immorality. Stop homosexuality. Stop lesbian-ism." Hecklers threw mud and water at him and knocked him to the ground—yet police arrested this old man, rather than his assailants, for a "breach of public order."

Homosexuals Are Dangerous to Children and Family

A fifth element of the homosexual agenda is the effort to get homo-sexual propaganda included in the curriculum of public schools. The intent of these efforts is obvious—to ensure that the next generation will grow up with an unquestioning acceptance of all the myths that the homosexual activists want young people to believe.

And a final element in this agenda is to redefine marriage and fam-ily altogether. They hope to achieve this by opening the door for homosexuals to adopt children and by legalizing same-sex marriage. If denied marriage in name, they hope to win virtually all the benefits and privileges of marriage through so-called civil unions or domestic partnerships. . . .

Lesbian activist Paula Ettelbrick, currently the executive director of the International Gay and Lesbian Human Rights Commission, has said that homosexuality "means pushing the parameters of sex, sexuality, and family, and in the process transforming the very fab-ric of society." In fact, homosexuality and homosexual civil marriage would rip the fabric of society in ways that may be difficult, if not impossible, to mend.

EVALUATING THE AUTHOR'S ARGUMENTS:

In the viewpoint you just read, author Peter Sprigg argues that homosexuality is immoral because it threatens the ideal form of the family: one man and one woman with children of their own. Do you agree or disagree with Sprigg's definition of the "ideal family"? Do you agree with Sprigg that all families should try to strive toward the "ideal," whether or not they succeed?

Homosexuality Is Not Immoral

Paul Varnell

"Psychologists and theologians have . . . sought [to] . . . debase, demean, pathologize, vilify or deny love between people of the same sex."

Paul Varnell is a journalist who writes on gay issues for the newspaper *Chicago Free Press*. In the following viewpoint, Varnell argues that homosexual love and relationships are neither better nor worse than heterosexual ones and certainly are not immoral. It is only because homosexuality is in the minority that it is thought of as different from heterosexuality. In fact, Varnell writes, homosexual love is the same as heterosexual love, with gay partners seeking the same qualities in their mates as their straight counterparts.

AS YOU READ, CONSIDER THE FOLLOWING QUESTIONS:

1. What would qualify someone to compare gay and straight love, in the opinion of the author?
2. What is the evidence someone might offer as to why same-sex love is superior to opposite-sex love?
3. What are the two opposite and contradictory errors heterosexuals make about gay relationships?

Paul Varnell, "Love Matters," *Chicago Free Press*, June 3, 2004.

Attitudes About Homosexuality

Should homosexuality be accepted by society?

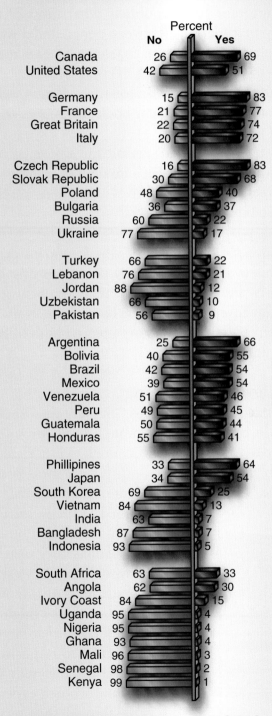

Percent

No   Yes

Country	No	Yes
Canada	26	69
United States	42	51
Germany	15	83
France	21	77
Great Britain	22	74
Italy	20	72
Czech Republic	16	83
Slovak Republic	30	68
Poland	48	40
Bulgaria	36	37
Russia	60	22
Ukraine	77	17
Turkey	66	22
Lebanon	76	21
Jordan	88	12
Uzbekistan	66	10
Pakistan	56	9
Argentina	25	66
Bolivia	40	55
Brazil	42	54
Mexico	39	54
Venezuela	51	46
Peru	49	45
Guatemala	50	44
Honduras	55	41
Phillipines	33	64
Japan	34	54
South Korea	69	25
Vietnam	84	13
India	63	7
Bangladesh	87	7
Indonesia	93	5
South Africa	63	33
Angola	62	30
Ivory Coast	84	15
Uganda	95	4
Nigeria	95	4
Ghana	93	4
Mali	96	3
Senegal	98	2
Kenya	99	1

Taken from: "Homosexuality Should Be Accepted by Society,"
Pew Global Attitudes Project, June 2003

In his book *The Broken Hearth*, conservative polemicist [someone who argues in opposition to others] William J. Bennett remarks that it is important to say publicly what most of us believe privately, namely that marriage between a man and a woman is in every way to be preferred to the marriage of two men or two women.

To which author and columnist Jonathan Rauch, who quotes Bennett's observation in his excellent book *Gay Marriage*, responds:

> I have to say, if the reader will permit me a moment of exasperation, that we homosexuals get a bit tired of being assured by heterosexuals that their loves and lives and unions are 'in every way' better than ours.

Indeed. Take love, for instance. One wonders how a person loudly proclaiming his own heterosexuality could possibly know that heterosexual love is better "in every way" than love between a gay or lesbian couple. Gay love might even be better—"in every way to be preferred." But unless someone had experienced both fully he could hardly have grounds for comparison.

Homosexual Love Is Not Wrong

But psychologists and theologians have "in every way" sought to elevate heterosexual love and debase, demean, pathologize, vilify or deny love between people of the same sex—reduce it to lust, claim it is fleeting, view it as somehow incomplete, or treat it as strictly self-regarding or "narcissistic." Since these claims are seldom argued, and when "argued" usually start with the desired conclusion built into the assumptions, they smack of a desperate defense of a weak position.

If qualities of love were to be ranked, someone might offer the counter claim that same-sex love is superior to opposite sex love because the different ways that men and women experience the world through their very different

FAST FACT

The number of gays and lesbians in the United States is estimated at 8.8 million.

bodies and hormonally influenced outlooks means they can hardly reach a degree of sympathetic understanding necessary for love.

Love Is Natural in All Forms

No doubt if heterosexuals were a long-stigmatized minority, a homosexual majority would think of heterosexual "love" as based primarily on lust or a depraved desire for exotically produced orgasms ("You do what?"), as shallow and doomed to failure because the partners are

Homosexual couples feel that the love they share is no different than that shared by straight couples and that it shouldn't be viewed as morally wrong.

"just too different to feel enduring love," as incomplete and lacking empathy, as rooted in a subconscious self-hatred or desire to identify with or become the other sex, etc., etc.

But in the end it is hard to think of any very persuasive reason why love—the emotional and erotic experience of feeling bonded to someone else—between people of the same sex should be different in nature or quality from love between people of the opposite sex. Love after all seems to be a natural human capacity and could hardly be said to differ in nature according to the sex of its object or the person who experiences it.

At its core, love seems to involve not exactly a "bonding to" another person, but a partial breakdown of the barriers between them so that each takes on the elements, concerns, the well-being of the other person and makes them part of the person's own being. Thus the empty feeling when couples separate or a long-term partner dies: part of oneself no longer exists and the person feels suddenly incomplete.

Love Means Finding an Opposite

It might seem, and may be true, that gays and lesbians have an initial advantage of interpersonal empathy because of their similar bodies and social conditioning. But even for gays and lesbians it seems safe to say that love, like sex, usually requires a greater or lesser degree of difference between the two people that makes them interesting, stimulating to each other.

What is involved in attraction, and ultimately love, is a desire to incorporate or associate with or "import" the desired qualities in the other person. Those need not be qualities a person himself lacks; they may be ones he already has but admires and desires more of.

Heterosexuals and their apologists [someone who defends an idea] used to make two opposite (and mutually contradictory) errors about gay relationships. Mapping gay relationships onto heterosexual ones, they assumed there would be a masculine and a feminine partner. But in fact it is more logical that gay men, most of them reasonably masculine, would be attracted to other masculine gay men. Having eroticized masculinity in the first place, they would reasonably look for it in a partner.

Partners Can Be Similar, Yet Different

But—and this was the opposite error—that did not mean that gay men were looking for someone exactly like themselves. Masculinity has numerous modalities or "flavors," intensities, and styles, and no man can embody more than a few. So a man may be attracted to someone who embodies other modalities, or ones close to his own but with a different personality or presentation.

As psychologist C.A. Tripp put it in his book *The Homosexual Matrix:*

> In less obvious examples, the contrast between partners may appear slight to an outside observer, but it is always there and constitutes the basis of the attraction. Notions to the effect that the homosexual is looking for some 'narcissistic' reflection of his own image are as mythical as was [Greek mythologial figure] Narcissus himself.

EVALUATING THE AUTHOR'S ARGUMENTS:

In the viewpoint you just read, author Paul Varnell bases his argument around the idea of mutual love. In the previous viewpoint, Peter Sprigg's argument is based around the idea of the strength of the family. In your opinion, which of these is more important when considering a relationship, gay or straight? Why?

Homosexuality Is a Choice

Yvette C. Schneider

"Scientists have not even come close to proving a genetic or biological cause for homosexuality."

Yvette Schneider is a policy analyst for the Family Research Council, a conservative social policy group. In the following viewpoint, Schneider argues that homosexuality is a choice that people make. There is no biological basis to homosexuality, she states, and there is no such thing as the "gay gene" that many homosexual people say they possess. Since there is no biological basis for homosexuality, gay people should be held responsible for their sexual orientation and the choices they make should be considered voluntary, Schneider writes.

AS YOU READ, CONSIDER THE FOLLOWING QUESTIONS:

1. To what other "dangerous" activities does the author compare homosexuality?
2. According to the poll Schneider cites, what percentage of people believes homosexuality is genetic? What percentage believes it is learned?
3. What have activists used as a "stamp of legitimacy" in seeking gay rights, according to the viewpoint?

Yvette C. Schneider, "The Gay Gene: Going, Going . . . Gone," Family Research Council, www.frc.org, April 24, 2006.

M any misconceptions exist about the supposedly inborn nature of complex behaviors such as homosexuality. Most of these are due to media reports that present scientific studies in selective sound bites.

In reality, no scientific studies show an inborn cause for any such complex behaviors. In this day of shirking responsibility and blaming anything but ourselves for our actions, claims that someone is genetically or chemically structured to engage in dangerous or antisocial activities find increasing appeal.

People have asserted that they cannot keep themselves from smoking, drinking, or even [committing] adultery, because they were born with uncontrollable proclivities. While it is true that we are born with fallen natures that incline us toward any number of vices, it is an error to contend that an inclination is "uncontrollable." We can make choices and are not hopelessly forced to engage in illicit or dangerous practices of any sort.

Many Believe Homosexuality Is Genetic

When the question of the origin of homosexuality arises, homosexual activists tend to resort to the often-heard refrain "I was born gay." There are even T-shirts sold at homosexual functions and bookstores that say, "Hey Mom, Thanks for the Genes." The idea that homosexuality is a predetermined condition that originates in the womb also has been increasingly embraced by society as a whole. A February 2000 Harris Poll of 1,010 randomly selected adults found that the number of people who believe "sexual orientation" "is more dependent on the genes you are born with" has increased 6 percent since 1995. Thirty-five percent of the people polled believe that homosexuality is "genetic," versus 29 percent who held that opinion in 1995. Fifty-two percent believe that "what you learn and experience" causes homosexuality, as opposed to 65 percent who believed that in 1995.

But what do we really know about the science of behavior? Not much. Scientific studies have done more to confirm the complexities of human behavior than they have to isolate specific causes. . . .

Some people believe that homosexuals choose their lifestyle rather than being born gay.

There Is No Gay Gene

Edward Stein, Ph.D., homosexual activist and author of *The Mismeasure of Desire: The Science, Theory, and Ethics of Sexual Orientation*, critically examines the research of [scientists Dean Hamer and Simon LeVay] that claims a biological origin to homosexuality. In an interview with the *Advocate* (a homosexual magazine), Stein said, "There are serious problems with the science itself. . . . My training had taught me that a lot of what was being said was, well, highly unscientific."

Stein also explains in his book that none of the researchers studying hypothesized biological origins of homosexuality has proven direct causation, although in some circumstances they claim to have done just that. [Stein states]

Genes in themselves cannot directly specify any behavior or psychological phenomenon. Instead, genes direct a particular pattern of RNA synthesis, which in turn may influence the development of psychological dispositions and the expression of behaviors.

There are necessarily many intervening pathways between a gene and a disposition or a behavior, and even more intervening variables between a gene and a pattern that involves both thinking and behaving. The terms 'gay gene' and 'homosexual gene' are, therefore, without meaning. No one has presented evidence in support of such a simple and direct link between genes and sexual orientation. . . .

Homosexuals Have a Choice

There is increasing debate among homosexual activists as to whether or not they should even be advocating the idea that homosexuality is genetic. It was once thought to be politically expedient to say, "I can't help my attractions. I was born this way." Stein told the *Advocate*,,

Many gay people want to use this research to promote gay rights. If gay people are 'born that way,' then discrimination against them must be wrong. . . . A gay or lesbian person's public identity, sexual behaviors, romantic relationships, or decisions to raise children are all choices. No theory suggests that these choices are genetic.

FAST FACT

Scientists estimate that approximately five percent of the total human population worldwide has a homosexual orientation.

Not only is the scientific research that tries to prove an inborn nature to homosexuality questionable, but the researchers also fail to take into account the existence of thousands of former homosexuals. If homosexuality were biologically determined, it would seem impossible for homosexuals to become heterosexual.

Homosexuals Can Change

Recently, Dr. Robert Spitzer, one of the men who helped change the American Psychiatric Association's opinion on homosexuality as a mental disorder in 1973, acknowledged that homosexuals can

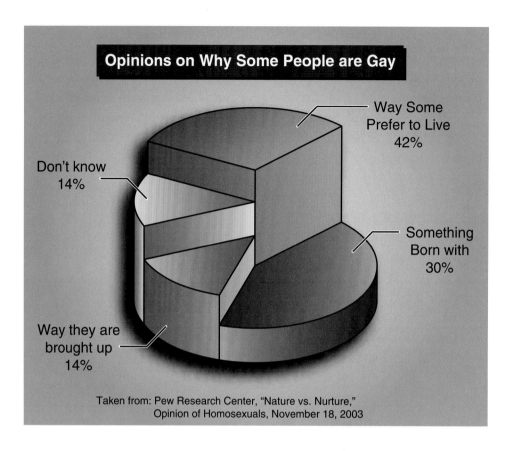

Opinions on Why Some People are Gay

Way Some Prefer to Live
42%

Don't know
14%

Something Born with
30%

Way they are brought up
14%

Taken from: Pew Research Center, "Nature vs. Nurture,"
Opinion of Homosexuals, November 18, 2003

become heterosexual. In an interview with *CitizenLink* online newsletter, Spitzer said, "The critics of this kind of therapy don't just argue that it is rarely effective; they argue that it's never effective."

Spitzer is interviewing former homosexuals who have left the homosexual lifestyle and have lost their attractions for the same sex. He said,

> What we're really trying to see is, 'Are there individuals who give a pretty convincing report that they have changed in a fundamental way their sexual orientation, and has it been sustained for many years? . . . I'm personally convinced that many of these individuals have maintained and made major changes in their sexual orientation.

Scientists have not even come close to proving a genetic or biological cause for homosexuality, yet homosexual activists continue to say that sexual activity between members of the same sex is "just the same" as race or gender. Using "biology" as a stamp of legitimacy, activists have pushed for special rights, from sex-partner subsidies to "gay marriage" to adoption. Without scientific evidence to support such claims, it is wrong and dangerously misleading to say that people are born homosexual and cannot change.

EVALUATING THE AUTHOR'S ARGUMENTS:

Yvette Schneider, author of the viewpoint you just read, identifies herself as a former lesbian who is now married to a man. Does knowing this alter your opinion of her argument? Explain why or why not.

Homosexuality Is Not a Choice

Cynthia Tucker

"Researchers theorize that sexual orien- tation . . . is determined so early in a child's for- mation that it cannot be considered a choice."

In the following viewpoint, author Cynthia Tucker argues that sexual orientation is not a choice that a person is free to make. Sexual preference is made up of both genes and environment, Tucker writes, and is formed at a very young age. People who are antigay choose to believe that homosexuality is a choice because it enables them to view gays as sinful. Gays suffer so much prejudice, Tucker argues, that it does not make sense that they would choose such a difficult life. Cynthia Tucker is a syndicated columnist and editor of the opinion section of the *Atlanta Journal-Constitution*.

AS YOU READ, CONSIDER THE FOLLOWING QUESTIONS:
1. According to Tucker, why would most parents of gay people dis- agree that homosexuality is a choice?
2. What is one consequence for parents who publicly demonstrate their love for their gay children?
3. How does Tucker describe homophobia?

Cynthia Tucker, "Homophobia a Cruel Choice," *Atlanta Journal-Constitution,* October 24, 2004.

B ecause [during the 2004 presidential campaign, Vice President] Dick Cheney and his wife, Lynne, managed to change the conversation about *homosexuality* to a contentious discussion of whether John Kerry smeared their daughter [who is lesbian], there

Some people suggest that the hostility and violence homosexuals face make it unlikely that they are choosing their gender preference.

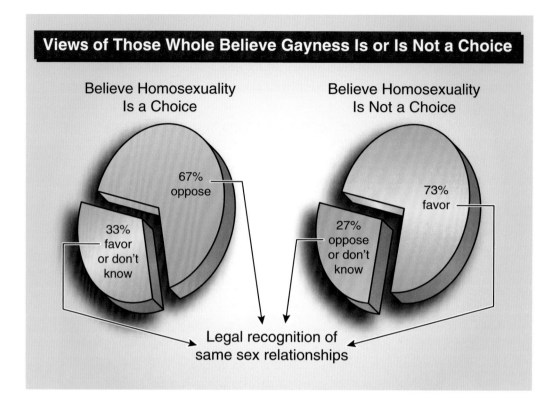

Views of Those Whole Believe Gayness Is or Is Not a Choice

Believe Homosexuality
Is a Choice

67%
oppose

33%
favor
or don't
know

Believe Homosexuality
Is Not a Choice

73%
favor

27%
oppose
or don't
know

Legal recognition of
same sex relationships

was little public discussion about the original question during [the] third [official] debate: Do you believe *homosexuality* is a choice?

If you want to condemn gays to hell, it helps to believe they have chosen a "lifestyle" based "simply on the premise of selfish hedonism," as Alan Keyes, the GOP [Republican Party] candidate for the Senate in Illinois, said of the Cheneys' lesbian daughter, Mary. (Interestingly, the Cheneys uttered not one word in public condemnation of Keyes. Could it be because Keyes is a Republican?) For people such as Keyes, *homosexuality* has to be viewed as *a choice*. Otherwise, it couldn't be a sin.

Being Gay Is Not a Choice

Science tends to dispute the reactionary [extremely conservative] Keyes. Researchers theorize that sexual orientation is determined by a complex interplay of factors—including environment, genes and hormones—and is determined so early in a child's formation that it cannot be considered a choice.

But there is a group of folks in a position to know even better than scientists—parents of gay and lesbian children. Many of them have struggled to understand and to support and love their children no matter what. They have worried about the bigotry their sons and daughters face every day. And they know their children would never have chosen to belong to the most despised group in America.

The Cheneys surely cannot believe their daughter "chose" to be gay.

"It took a lot of time and a lot of reading" for Frances Cunningham to become comfortable with her daughter's homosexuality. "When she told me, I think I would have been more prepared for her to tell me she had two heads or three feet," she said. But, looking back, "I know this has always been part of her."

Cunningham now says she has not only deep love but also admiration for her daughter, Kecia, a Decatur [Georgia] commissioner.

Hard for Families to Accept

Said Craig Washington, a black gay activist, "I think it was more difficult for my father. . . . I think there is a particular challenge to a black man when his son presents as gay. I think they first think, 'Well, what did I do wrong?' But gradually he came to accept my sexuality as not a failure or a flaw but just as fact."

Having his parents' support, Washington said, is "a blessing. . . . I think in a lot of ways they demonstrate what it is to love someone beyond their comfort. . . . To love somebody even when they haven't turned out to be what they expected."

Unlike the Cheneys, who remain among the royalty of reactionary politics, many parents who publicly demonstrate their love for gay or lesbian children find themselves alienated from family, church and community. That is especially true for black families, given the vile homophobia rampant in black America.

Homophobia Is Cruel

It's because of fears of alienation that E. asked that her name not be used, even as she spoke of her love and support for her son. "Not all of our family members know. . . . His father still has a very hard time with this. He just doesn't want to hear about it."

Indeed, she says, her son could not at first acknowledge his sexual orientation even to her, denying that he was gay each time she asked. "Finally, I said, 'If you can't tell your mother, who could you tell?'"

As she has sought to learn more, E. said, she has heard young black adults who are gay or lesbian speak of their fears of living openly, of being rejected by their parents, aunts and uncles. "That made me think we're just not embracing our children," she said.

Homophobia is the last acceptable prejudice in America. And its perpetrators comfort themselves with the thought that they are simply castigating a group of sinful sexual bohemians—instead of mocking and vilifying the lives of people who happen to love someone of the same sex.

The bigots' self-justification doesn't make their bigotry any less cruel. It never has.

EVALUATING THE AUTHOR'S ARGUMENTS:

In the viewpoint you just read, author Cynthia Tucker argues that gay people have no choice as to whether or not they are gay. In the previous viewpoint, Yvette Schneider takes the opposite stance, declaring homosexuality a conscious choice that gay people make. After considering both arguments, which do you agree with more? Why?

Gay People Can Be a Threat to Children

Linda Harvey

> "When people have views supporting homosexuality, they should not be involved with youth in any way, period."

Linda Harvey is a member of the conservative family-values organization Concerned Women for America. She is also the founder of Mission America, a group dedicated to exposing homosexuality in schools. In the following viewpoint, Harvey argues that modern youth are under pressure from popular media and culture to accept homosexuality as normal and good. If permitted around children, Harvey writes, gay adults contribute to this attitude, helping to create "new homosexuals." Children must be shielded from these influences and people, she states, in order to protect their innocence.

AS YOU READ, CONSIDER THE FOLLOWING QUESTIONS:

1. What influences form the identitiy of the average American adolescent like Josh, according to the author?
2. Name two reasons cited by the author why people who support homosexuality should not be involved with youth.
3. Name three possible circumstances that can cause a young person to suspect he or she might be gay, according to the viewpoint.

Linda Harvey, "Fairy Tales Don't Come True," Concerned Women for America, www.cwfa.org, February 13, 2006.

J osh is 13 and, like many kids his age, he's often unhappy. Everything about his life is uncertain. He's only 5 feet 4 inches tall, and many of the girls in his middle-school class are taller. He has no idea how his body will end up. Will he be tall, short, plain, handsome? He's slightly overweight and hasn't found a sport he excels in. He only has two or three close friends. Sometimes his voice changes an entire octave, up or down, at a moment's notice. He's an average student, and he sometimes dreads going to school because it doesn't interest him much. . . .

In other words, Josh is a lot like many American adolescents. His family has only casual ties to a church, and his parents consider themselves moderate politically, when they have time or interest to think about it.

Josh's standards are being formed largely not by parents of high character, but by the American culture, including television, his public school and the Internet. That's where he developed a keen curiosity about sex, and it's also where he gets his information and values. And his values right now are leaning toward believing he might be a homosexual.

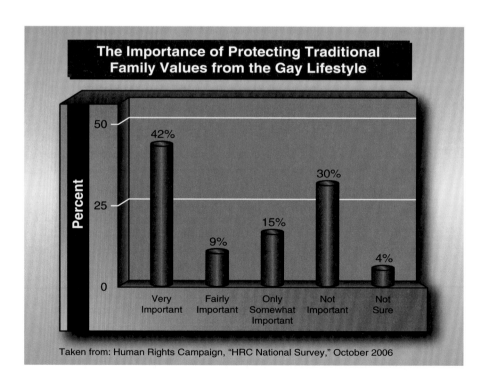

The Importance of Protecting Traditional Family Values from the Gay Lifestyle

Taken from: Human Rights Campaign, "HRC National Survey," October 2006

Influence at School

He has absorbed information at school that most homosexuals are victims of terrible discrimination, even sometimes violence, so "good" people are those who accept homosexuality, bisexuality and gender changes. Most of his teachers believe that homosexuality isn't a choice and that students with same-sex attractions should just accept them. At least three separate school offerings left him with these ideas: a book on different types of families his teacher read aloud in third grade; a sixth grade anti-bias and "tolerance" unit, and an assignment in his literature class where he read a novel about teen boys exploring homosexuality. . . .

If he's a homosexual, he thinks, this would explain why he craves being close to other boys. Sometimes he thinks it's just because he never sees his dad, but he's not sure. Also, girls aren't interested in him. Girls seem like a lot of trouble. It would be so much more fun to be physical with someone who likes the same things he does—Playstation, movies and role-playing games. And having sex without any thoughts of pregnancy, commitment and all that serious stuff. Wouldn't that be great? Besides, he was physically aroused looking at "gay" porn sites. Doesn't that prove he must be a homosexual? . . .

Children Are Being Exploited

Josh is not a real person, but a composite of different teens I have learned about over the 10 years I've been researching this issue. The tale is tragically similar; only the names change. The turbulence of many American families coupled with the usual challenges of childhood and adolescence present the opportunity for depravity to take hold in the young mind

FAST FACT

In 2000, the Supreme Court upheld a ruling stating that the Boy Scouts of America could prohibit homosexual men from being troop leaders.

and spirit. Children are being deliberately exploited at a time when they are extremely vulnerable, and virtually no one, it seems, is paying attention. Opportunities exist for them to get involved in life-changing behaviors like homosexuality before their parents have any idea. . . .

Some people fear that homosexuals may have a negative influence on children with whom they have frequent contact.

Why are we allowing this to happen? The reason is simple: As a society, we aren't protecting our kids from danger. When we turn on the television, allow them to use the Internet, send them off to school or, in some cases, when we take them to certain churches, we are exposing them to harm.

We've opened up access to our children by those who are not trustworthy.

When people have views supporting homosexuality, they should not be involved with youth in any way, period. Because they:

- will provide inaccurate, misleading information to kids;
- may limit a student's opportunity to hear warnings about the behavior;
- may advocate or model inappropriate behavior;
- may be directly involved in the molestation of kids themselves; or
- may be in a position to allow others to do so.

People Who Choose Homosexuality

These warnings beg a very serious question: Can people, children in this case, become homosexuals by exposure to certain ideas and behavior? In other words, can a person who would not otherwise become homosexual start the behavior, come to prefer it and form a habitual addiction?

Can a society create more homosexuals? The answer quite clearly is *yes*. . . .

People, especially the young, can be seduced into homosexual behavior and have their identities molded around the homosexual lifestyle through a combination of persuasion and circumstances that may include the following:

- being convinced homosexuality is acceptable;
- reading or viewing explicit homosexual pornography;
- having a close relationship with a peer who is practicing homosexuality;
- admiring an older teacher or mentor who is homosexual;
- attending homosexual social venues (a "gay" club, bar, church youth group);
- being homosexually molested;

- having parents who espouse homosexuality or engage in homo-sexual activism;
- lacking strong ties to a church that remains faithful to the historic Christian faith, and hostility toward traditional views. . . .

The level of brainwashing of young people today is astounding. They are trained to uncritically accept that a certain population segment will inevitably be "GLBT" ("gay, lesbian, bisexual or transgendered"). They hear over and over that any opposition to the practice of homosexuality arises only out of hate and ignorance. This propaganda is thorough and frightening because it envelops otherwise keen young minds. . . .

There is a dearth of ammunition for debate in the youth marketplace of ideas, and so darkness is overcoming our children because we refuse to bring them light.

Imagining a Gay Man's Future

So what becomes of all the Joshes out there? They seldom hear another viewpoint; they are seldom approached by Christian peers who will show them a different way. It's not that our Christian kids don't want to; they don't have enough information and are too intimidated to challenge the easily provoked pro-"gay" advocates.

So, Josh will probably go ahead and attend a local "gay" community group; then in high school, join the high school "GSA" ("gay"-straight alliance, the name of many homosexual clubs). He probably will pair up with an older homosexual and begin homosexual sex. His parents, anxious to be politically correct, won't object and will eventually come to accept his "lifestyle."

Josh's future probably holds a revolving door of sexual contacts, with his first visit to a clinic to be treated for a sexually transmitted disease [STD] at around age 17. Then, if he's typical, he'll be treated annually for an STD of some type. Oh, and all those middle school insecurities over appearance have been dispelled. He's turned into a drop-dead gorgeous young man, but he has no interest in the appreciative glances of young women. He's too much in demand at the "gay" bars and bathhouses.

Difficulties for Josh

He is already drinking heavily, smoking and doing recreational drugs. Somewhere along the line, he'll have several longer-term boyfriends, and may even move in with one or two of them. Their break-ups will happen after six months or a year, and be spectacular events punctuated with drama, screaming fights and threats of self-harm, contributing to the high rates of domestic violence cited for "gay" males.

He will go to a counselor for treatment of depression, anxiety or an eating disorder. Seeking some peace and stability, he'll join a "gay"-friendly [church]. Along the way, he may well become HIV-positive [carrying the virus that transmits AIDS]. In his 30s, he will start to have relationships with boys who are 16 and 17, just as someone did when he was a teen. He may even transmit the HIV virus to one or more of them.

Josh is likely to die early, probably before 55 and very likely in his 40s. His grandmother will cry at his funeral, knowing he would have made a great father and even grandfather. But it won't happen for him.

This was happiness? This is freedom? Why can't Josh be told the rest of the story before it's too late?

EVALUATING THE AUTHOR'S ARGUMENTS:

Throughout the viewpoint you just read, author Linda Harvey uses the word "homosexual" to refer to people who are attracted to those of the same sex. John Corvino uses the word "gay." Harvey generally opposes homosexual relationships while Corvino generally supports them. After reading both viewpoints, consider how the word choice influences the meaning of each argument. Which word do you prefer? Why?

Gay People Are Not a Particular Threat to Children

John Corvino

"Research shows that gay men are no more likely than straight men to molest children."

In the following viewpoint, author John Corvino argues that society unfairly views gay men as more likely to be child molesters or pedophiles than straight men, and thus assumes they will be dangerous to children. Corvino makes reference to a scandal in which congressional representative Mark Foley was caught sending sexually explicit text messages to teenage male congressional pages. People often assume, Corvino writes, that when one gay man behaves badly, that all gay men are more likely to do so. This is unfair, he says, because no one makes the same assumptions about straight men who are child molesters or who are otherwise dangerous to children. John Corvino is a writer and gay rights activist who teaches philosophy at Wayne State University in Michigan.

John Corvino, "The Pedophilia Smear," *Between the Lines*, October 19, 2006.

AS YOU READ, CONSIDER THE FOLLOWING QUESTIONS:
1. Why do mental health professionals recognize that most men who molest boys are not typically "gay" by definition?
2. Why should people avoid lumping together those who are attracted to adults of the same sex and those who are attracted to children of the same sex, according to the author?
3. Identify and explain the "double standard" to which the author refers.

The scandal involving [U.S. congressional representative] Mark Foley sending sexually explicit text messages to 16- and 17-year-old former congressional pages has resurrected the ugly stereotype of gays as pedophiles. I am no longer surprised when I hear this sort of garbage from the [conservative social values group] Family Research Council. But when the *Wall Street Journal* links the two by criticizing those "who tell us that the larger society must be tolerant of private lifestyle choices, and certainly must never leap to conclusions about gay men and young boys," it makes me nervous—not to mention angry.

Gay Men Are Not Necessarily Child Molesters

First, a little bit of perspective on the scandal driving this. The young men whom Foley courted were 16 and 17—not adults, but not children either. The age of consent in Washington, D.C. (and many other places) is 16. Issues of potential harassment aside, had Foley had [consensual] sex with these young men in Washington, it would have been perfectly legal.

Yet as far as we know, he did not have sex with them: he e-mailed and text-messaged them. Foley may be a jerk, a hypocrite, a creep—even a harasser—but there's no evidence that he qualifies as a child molester.

Research shows that gay men are no more likely than straight men to molest children. Moreover, mental health professionals are virtually unanimous in recognizing that most males who molest boys are not "gay" by any reasonable definition of that term: they have no interest in other adult males and often have successful relationships with adult females. This fact should not be surprising, because a young boy is at

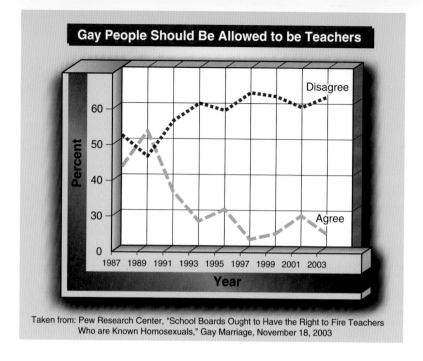

Gay People Should Be Allowed to be Teachers

Taken from: Pew Research Center, "School Boards Ought to Have the Right to Fire Teachers Who are Known Homosexuals," Gay Marriage, November 18, 2003

least as different a sexual object from an adult male as an adult female is. In other words, it's one thing to be attracted to adults of the same sex, it's quite another to be attracted to children of either sex. Lumping these categories together not only maligns innocent people; it distracts us from the real threats to children.

Gay Men Should Not Be Restricted

But it gets worse. For the pedophilia myth is yet another case of right-wingers arguing from what is not true to what does not follow. Suppose, purely for the sake of argument, there were a higher incidence of child molestation among homosexual males than heterosexual males. Should gay men no longer be permitted to be teachers? Pediatricians? Day care providers?

Be careful how you answer. Because one thing the research does clearly show is that men are far more likely to be child molesters than women. So if you think gay men should be restricted from these positions under the hypothetical (and false) assumption that they are more likely to be child molesters than straight men, you should conclude—in the actual, non-hypothetical world—that straight men should be thus restricted, and that all such jobs should go to lesbians and straight females. We know for a fact that men pose a higher risk of child molestation and other crimes than women do.

Making General Inferences

Yet somehow, when it comes to straight men, we are able to distinguish between those behaving well and those behaving badly. This double standard was quite apparent as the Foley scandal broke. Around the same time, admitted heterosexual Charles Carl Roberts walked into an Amish schoolhouse in Pennsylvania and fatally shot five female students. It turns out that Roberts told his wife that he had previously molested young girls. Yet no one took this story as tarnishing heterosexuality. No one concluded, "Aha! Can't trust straights." That would be a foolish inference.

James Dale was an Eagle Scout leader until the Boy Scouts barred him from the organization when they learned he was gay.

Just as foolish as making inferences about all gays from the case of Mark Foley—who, it is worth repeating, did not even have sex with the pages (as far as we know), much less kill anyone.

The point is that some gays, just like some straights, behave badly. This is not news. Nor is it a reason to draw blanket inferences about gays.

Some years ago I was invited to Nevada to debate a Mormon minister on same-sex marriage. One of his central arguments—I am not making this up—was that we should not support same-sex marriage because research shows that gays are more likely to engage in domestic violence than straights. I had never heard of the studies he cited, so it was difficult to challenge him directly on his sources. Instead, I asked, "So, because some asshole beats his husband, I'm supposed to stop loving mine? And everyone else should stop supporting me in my loving, non-abusive relationship? Is that what you're arguing?"

He never had an answer to that.

EVALUATING THE AUTHOR'S ARGUMENTS:

The authors of the two previous viewpoints, John Corvino and Linda Harvey, disagree on whether gay people are by definition dangerous to children. However, Corvino focuses his argument around the issue of child molestation and Harvey focuses hers on children who feel they might be gay. Taking into account these distinctions, with which argument do you agree? Explain your answer.

Chapter 2

Should Gay People Have the Same Rights as Straight People?

We are your neighbors.©
And...we are gay.

www.georgiaequality.org

000021　　ClearChannel

Gays are finding new ways to appeal to people in their quest for equality.

There Is Little Need for the Gay Rights Movement Anymore

Dale Carpenter

"[We have] entered what I expect will be the end stage of the gay-rights movement."

Dale Carpenter is a professor of law at the University of Minnesota. In the following viewpoint, he argues that the gay rights movement has virtually achieved its basic end goal: full acceptance of gays and gay relationships in mainstream society. Same-sex marriage was the last goal, Carpenter writes, and the country seems poised to accept it. Therefore, the gay rights movement is no longer necessary in the twenty-first century.

Editor's note: In June 2007, the Massachusetts legislature voted 151 to 45 against a proposed amendment to define marriage as between a man and a woman. Fifty votes were needed to place the amendment before voters on the November 2008 ballot.

Dale Carpenter, "The End of Gay Rights," *Bay Area Reporter,* May 27, 2004.

AS YOU READ, CONSIDER THE FOLLOWING QUESTIONS:
1. What time period does Carpenter identify as the starting and ending points for the Emergence stage of the gay rights movement?
2. What was the predominant American reaction to the AIDS epidemic?
3. What specific event signals the end of the gay rights movement as a whole, according to Carpenter?

T he movement for gay equality in America has come in four basic stages. Each of these stages made a distinct contribution; each was marked by its own missteps; each provoked stiff resistance; each suffered stinging defeats; but each ultimately advanced the cause and prepared the way for the next stage. With the recognition of same-sex marriages in Massachusetts [in 2004]—the first time a state has done so—we have entered the final stage of the gay-rights movement.

The first stage of the movement covered roughly the middle of the 20th century up to the time of the Stonewall riot [a series of violent conflicts between gays and police officers] in New York in June 1969. We might call this stage Emergence, since it marked the moment that homosexuals began to emerge from the closet and to organize politically for the first time.

The atmosphere in the country during the Emergence period was harshly repressive. Homosexuality was considered not just sinful, but a mental disorder. All 50 states had sodomy laws directed and enforced primarily against gay sex. Raids on gay bars were common. Known homosexuals were forbidden in many states from obtaining professional and business licenses.

In the face of this discrimination, a few extraordinarily courageous individuals declared that homosexuals were perfectly

> **FAST FACT**
>
> The modern gay rights movement is usually considered to have begun with the Stonewall Rebellion on June 28, 1969, in which police raided the Stonewall Inn, a gay bar in New York City, and clashed with the patrons, sparking rioting.

normal. They formed political and educational groups like the Mattachine Society and the Daughters of Bilitis. During this period the American Law Institute recommended eliminating sodomy laws, and Illinois became the first state to do so, in 1961.

The Liberating Stage of Gay Rights

Stonewall marked a new and more radical stage in the gay-rights movement. We might call this stage Liberation, since the gay movement appropriated the rhetoric and methods of other liberation movements for women and racial minorities. Liberation is also an appropriate moniker for this second stage, because the movement emphasized separation from mainstream American society and institutions through unbridled sexual freedom and revolutionary critiques of existing customs and ways of living.

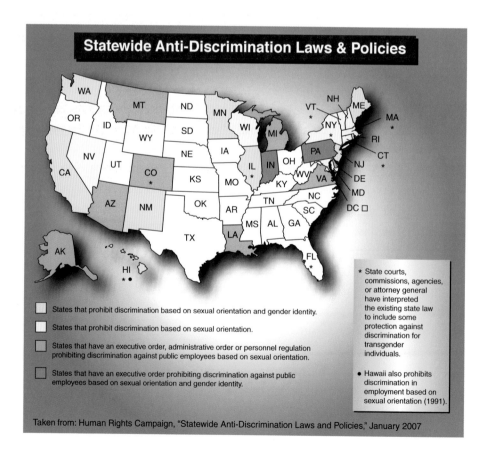

Statewide Anti-Discrimination Laws & Policies

☐ States that prohibit discrimination based on sexual orientation and gender identity.

☐ States that prohibit discrimination based on sexual orientation.

☐ States that have an executive order, administrative order or personnel regulation prohibiting discrimination against public employees based on sexual orientation.

☐ States that have an executive order prohibiting discrimination against public employees based on sexual orientation and gender identity.

* State courts, commissions, agencies, or attorney general have interpreted the existing state law to include some protection against discrimination for transgender individuals.

• Hawaii also prohibits discrimination in employment based on sexual orientation (1991).

Taken from: Human Rights Campaign, "Statewide Anti-Discrimination Laws and Policies," January 2007

Work environments are becoming friendlier to gays as seen at the annual Out & Equal Workplace Summit in Minneapolis which included companies like Best Buy, Target, and IBM.

During the second stage of the gay-rights movement, the American Psychiatric Association removed homosexuality from its official list of mental disorders, many more states eliminated their sodomy laws, gay publications and organizations mushroomed, the first openly gay officials were elected, and a few localities banned discrimination on the basis of sexual orientation. . . .

Yet the second stage engendered a ferocious backlash, led by a newly self-conscious movement of social conservatives now known as the religious right. [Antigay activist] Anita Bryant infamously led successful drives to repeal gay-rights ordinances in places like Miami [Florida] and St. Paul [Minnesota].

The Effects of the AIDS Epidemic

The heady and optimistic second stage of the gay-rights movement ended with the onset of the AIDS epidemic in the early 1980s. AIDS soon sapped almost the entire energy of the movement. Gay advocates shifted from emphasizing freedom and separation to emphasizing caring, responsibility, community, and commitment—the preconditions for the development of a marriage ethic. At the same time, the brutal process of dying from a disease identified almost entirely with gay men brought many homosexuals out of the closet for the first time. The protest group ACT-UP, whose antics were sometimes childish and counter-productive, transformed the American medical establishment to be more responsive to patients' needs for care and lifesaving drugs.

While some Americans responded to AIDS by calling for quarantines, the predominant reaction was one of sympathy and support. We could call the third stage of the gay-rights movement Tolerance, since Americans now opposed many forms of discrimination yet remained convinced that homosexuality was morally wrong.

During the third stage, many more civil rights laws were passed, corporate America led the way to the equal treatment of gay couples, and sodomy laws were finally vanquished. Gay couples began to demand benefits, leading to the creation of private and public domestic partnerships and, toward the end of the third stage, civil unions in Vermont. Still, there were reverses, including the codification of the military's gay ban and a federal ban on recognizing gay marriages.

The End Stage of Gay Rights

On May 17, 2004, the day Massachusetts began recognizing same-sex marriages, we entered what I expect will be the end stage of the gay-rights movement.

As in each stage of the gay-rights movement before this one, gay advocates will be guilty of excesses and will suffer serious setbacks.

Beginning November [2004] we are going to be plastered in a series of antigay-marriage initiatives on state ballots around the country. Gay marriage will temporarily win a battle here and there in a few courts, but will overwhelmingly lose. For a time, legislatures will bottle up or defeat gay-marriage bills even in gay-friendly states like California.

Gay marriage may even lose its toehold in Massachusetts come November 2006, when citizens there may vote on a state constitutional amendment. But I doubt it, and even if we lose in Massachusetts, gay marriage will resurface somewhere before long. Having seen that gay marriage causes no harm and brings much joy, Americans will allow it, by fits and starts to sweep the country.

By the time that happens, perhaps 30 years from now, the need for an organized gay-rights movement in this country will be gone. There will still be bigotry and ignorance to fight, in America and around the world, but the heavy political and legal lifting will have been done.

History can't be written before it happens, and there is nothing inevitable about progress. But, if it turns out as I expect, this final phase should be called Acceptance, since it will end in gays' full inclusion in the nation's legal and social life.

EVALUATING THE AUTHOR'S ARGUMENTS:

The author of the preceding viewpoint, Dale Carpenter, identifies himself as a gay man. Carpenter argues that the gay rights movement is no longer necessary because it has achieved most of its goals. Does Carpenter's identity make his argument more or less convincing, in your opinion? How would you view his argument if he identified himself as a straight man?

The Gay Rights Movement Is Still Necessary

Matt Foreman

"The orchestrated campaign to deny us jobs, family recognition, children, and housing is immoral."

Matt Foreman is the executive director of the National Gay and Lesbian Task Force, a prominent gay rights advocacy group. In the following viewpoint, Foreman argues that gays are increasingly experiencing prejudice from what he calls the "Anti-Gay Industry." Gays must stand up for their rights, he declares, and defend themselves, rather than blaming themselves for civil rights losses. Mainstream acceptance of gays is far from achieved, Foreman writes, and gay agitation is the solution.

AS YOU READ, CONSIDER THE FOLLOWING QUESTIONS:

1. According to Foreman, what must gays do to reframe the debate on the gay rights movement?
2. How many anti-marriage state constitutional amendments does the author identify in the viewpoint?
3. Why do people who generally support equal rights for all tolerate gay discrimination, according to Foreman?

Matt Foreman, "Discrimination Is Immoral. Enough Said," *The Empty Closet,* May 11, 2005.

I'm hearing both gay and straight people say that the long string of losses we've faced at the polls [especially in November 2004] around marriage equality are really our own fault; our community pushed too hard and too fast, they argue. The prominent theme being generated is that we have failed to "educate" the public about who we really are and get beyond the stereotypes of leather people, butch dykes, circuit boys and drag queens—and that it is now our obligation to reintroduce ourselves to the American people. I also repeatedly hear that it's up to us to reframe the terms of the debate away from "moral values" to simpler concepts, such as fairness, which polls indicate resonate most with the public.

Fight Against Unfairness

I disagree. This is nothing more than the blame-the-victim mentality afflicting our nation generally and the lesbian, gay, bisexual, and transgender (LGBT) movement specifically.

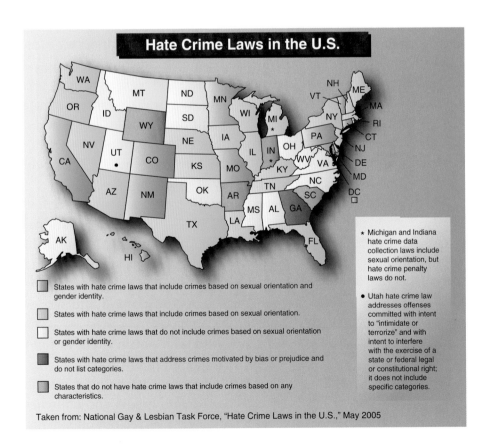

Hate Crime Laws in the U.S.

* Michigan and Indiana hate crime data collection laws include sexual orientation, but hate crime penalty laws do not.

• Utah hate crime law addresses offenses committed with intent to "intimidate or terrorize" and with intent to interfere with the exercise of a state or federal legal or constitutional right; it does not include specific categories.

☐ States with hate crime laws that include crimes based on sexual orientation and gender identity.

☐ States with hate crime laws that include crimes based on sexual orientation.

☐ States with hate crime laws that do not include crimes based on sexual orientation or gender identity.

☐ States with hate crime laws that address crimes motivated by bias or prejudice and do not list categories.

☐ States that do not have hate crime laws that include crimes based on any characteristics.

Taken from: National Gay & Lesbian Task Force, "Hate Crime Laws in the U.S.," May 2005

Rather than reframing the debate away from moral values, we must embrace them. Or more precisely, the utter immorality of the escalating attacks against LGBT people. And, equally, the utter immorality in the failure of so many people of good will to stand with us. It is time for us to seize the moral high ground and state unambiguously that anti-gay discrimination in any form is immoral.

Webster's defines discrimination as "unfair treatment of a person or group on the basis of prejudice." By any measure, LGBT people are targets of discrimination in employment, housing, and public accommodations. FBI [Federal Bureau of Investigation] statistics show that more people are being murdered because of their sexual orientation than for any other bias reason. Our young people are still routinely bullied in schools. The examples of injustices in the area of partner and family recognition are too many to list.

No thinking or feeling person can deny these realities, which, as always, fall hardest on LGBT people of color and those who are poor.

Gay Prejudice Rising

But, alarmingly, rather than seeing a groundswell of support for measures to combat these injustices, the opposite is occurring. In Congress and in statehouses nationwide, it's rhetorical and legislative open season on LGBT people. For example, [since August 2004] anti-marriage state constitutional amendments were put on the ballot in 14 states, 10 of which also prohibit the recognition of any form of relationship between people of the same gender. It's likely another 12 states will have similar measures on the ballot [by 2008].

Nothing like this has happened since the Constitution was ratified in 1791—essentially a national referendum inviting the public to vote to deprive a small minority of Americans of rights the majority takes for granted and sees as fundamental.

And who's been there to fight these amendments? Basically us, the very minority under attack. Mainstream media and churches are largely silent to our opponents'

FAST FACT

In thirty-three states, it is legal to fire someone based on their sexual orientation.

lies. Most progressive organizations and political campaigns, mean-while, steer clear. There have been sterling exceptions, but they have been few and far between.

Society Tolerates Gay Prejudice

Many people who see themselves as supporters of equal rights for all tolerate this because they believe prejudice on the basis of sexual orientation is profoundly different than that based on race or religion—that it comes from an understandable disapproval of our behavior—not on some "immutable characteristic." Homosexual behavior, they feel, is "unnatural" (doesn't the Bible say so?). Pundits say there is an "ick" factor—that the thought of gay sex revolts non-gay people, and that this seemingly innate reaction is proof there is something wrong with homosexuality.

This rationale is hardly unique to gay people. Scholars point to comparable "ick" sentiments about Irish immigrants in the 1880s, and describe how in preceding generations sexual ideology was used to strengthen control over slaves and to justify the taking of Native American lands, and that for centuries Jews were associated with disease and urban degeneration.

Fact is, there is no justification for anti-gay prejudice; the "justifications" for it are as unfounded as those used to support the second-class treatment of other minorities in past generations.

Gays Must Stand Up for Themselves

So, what needs to be done?

First, everyone must realize that when straight people say gay people should not have the freedom to marry, they are saying we are not as good or deserving as they are. It's that simple, no matter how one attempts to sugarcoat it.

This is unacceptable—and it is immoral.

Second, while we should talk to straight people honestly about our lives, we must flatly reject the notion that we are somehow to blame for all of this because we have not effectively communicated our "stories" to others. Fundamentally, it is not our job to prove to others that we can be good neighbors, good parents, and that gee whiz, we're actually people too.

Third, equality will remain elusive if we keep relying on intellectualized arguments or by dryly cataloguing, for example, each of the 1,138 federal rights and responsibilities we are forced to forgo due to marriage inequality.

The other side goes for the gut; it's now our turn.

Many people believe that the gay rights movement should remain strong until gays share equal rights with straight people.

There Is a Need to Fight

In this vein, we must put others on the spot to stand up and fight for us. As the cascade of lies pours forth from the Anti-Gay Industry, morality demands that non-gay people speak out with the same vehemence as they would if it was another minority under attack. Ministers and rabbis must be challenged with the question, "Where is your voice?" Elected officials who meet with and attend events of the Anti-Gay Industry, must be met with the challenge, "How can you do that!? How is that public service?"

The orchestrated campaign to deny us jobs, family recognition, children, and housing is immoral. Silently bearing witness to this discrimination is immoral.

America is in the midst of another ugly chapter in its struggle with the forces of bigotry. People of good will can either rise up to speak for lesbian, gay, bisexual and transgender Americans, or look back upon themselves 20 years from now with deserved shame.

EVALUATING THE AUTHOR'S ARGUMENTS:

Matt Foreman, the author of the viewpoint you just read, compares prejudice against gay people to that experienced by Irish immigrants, Native Americans, and Jews at various points in American history. What are the similarities and differences between gay people and the other groups Foreman names? Do you agree that this is a fair comparison? Why or why not?

Gay People Should Be Allowed to Adopt Children

Dennis Patrick

> *We have heard people say that our children are going to be "confused." Our children are not confused. They know that they are safe, secure and loved.*

In this viewpoint, Dennis Patrick argues that gay parents should be permitted to adopt children. He promotes the image of a loving gay-parented household by using his own as an example. Patrick outlines the discrimination and accusations he and his family have had to endure, and he demonstrates why those accusations have been misplaced. Many of the children Patrick and his partner have fostered and adopted over the years came from dysfunctional and abusive heterosexual households, and he contends that their past home environments deserve criticism, but their present situations with loving, gay parents do not. Dennis Patrick is a professor and an activist working to bring about positive legal changes for domestic partnership benefits and same-sex marriages.

Dennis Patrick, "A Father's Day Wish List from a Gay Dad." *The Progressive*, June 12, 2007.

AS YOU READ, CONSIDER THE FOLLOWING QUESTIONS:
  1. Why was his father-in-law disapproving of and uninvolved in Dennis Patrick's family?
  2. How does Patrick describe the lives of his fostered and adopted children from before they joined his family?
  3. Rather than changing his own family situation, what does Patrick believe is the solution to end the teasing of his children?

My father-in-law passed away this month [June 2007]. My heart goes out to his son and his four daughters as they cope with this loss.

Our own four sons, who are 11, 8, 7 and 5 years old, never met their grandfather, even though he lived less than two hours away. When we sent him photos of the children, they were promptly returned with a brief note stating, "These are not my grandchildren. I pray to God that you will come to your senses." The mistake we made, in his opinion, was the fact that his only son and I are an openly gay couple.

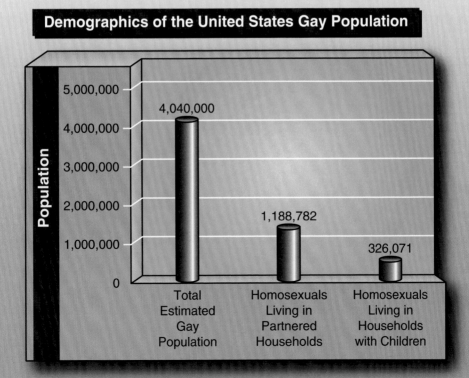

Demographics of the United States Gay Population

Taken from: "Estimated United States Population," United States Census Bureau, 2000

My partner and I have been together for almost 10 years, and for the last six of them, we have been licensed foster parents. During that time we have fostered 15 children, ranging in age from eight months to 17 years. This includes our four sons.

As gay dads, my partner, our children and I have all encountered discrimination—both within and outside our family.

We have heard people say that we are abducting "innocent" children. Sadly, the children we have fostered and adopted did not have the chance for the normal, carefree childhoods that many other kids experience. Our children had been physically and sexually abused. They had been neglected and abandoned. They had experienced homelessness. They had witnessed drug addiction, alcohol addiction and domestic violence. They had parents who are incarcerated.

Ironically, they were born into two-parent, heterosexual families, the very kind of traditional family that is often referred to as the ideal family form.

We have heard people say that our children are going to be "confused." Our children are not confused. They know that they are safe, secure and loved. If anything, they are confused about why their birth parents, who were supposed to protect them and keep them safe, hurt and abused them.

We have heard people say that our family is "immoral." I respectfully disagree with their interpretation of the Bible. We are actively involved and accepted in our church community, where I am the Christian Education director and teach Sunday School to second-through-fifth graders.

We have heard people say that our children will be teased and ostracized because they have gay dads. That may be true. We are teaching our children how to respond to this teasing. But we believe the solution is for other parents to teach their children not to tease and bully those who are different from them.

Many believe that gay couples are able to provide a loving and stable environment for children if they are allowed to adopt.

We have heard people say that every child needs a mother and a father. When they say that, they often mean that all children need warm, nurturing parents who can offer unconditional support and love. My partner and I give those things to our children.

Sometimes they mean that our boys need caring adult females in their lives. We agree, and that is why we have made sure that our sons are surrounded by a loving network of grandmothers, aunts and close friends.

Here is my Father's Day wish list.

I wish an end to this kind of discrimination and prejudice.

I wish openly gay and lesbian parents could foster and adopt in all 50 states.

I wish there were more second-parent adoption laws so children in gay and lesbian families would have the security of two legal parents.

I wish there were more states and companies offering domestic partner benefits so workers could have more flexibility in caring for their families.

Sometimes it is frustrating and tiring to experience discrimination and prejudice as a gay parent. But then I look at the paper heart our 8-year-old son gave us last year for Father's Day. On the front he wrote, "I love you Daddy and Papa. You are the best dads in the whole world."

That love makes it all worthwhile.

EVALUATING THE AUTHOR'S ARGUMENTS:

Patrick believes that gay couples should be permitted to adopt children. In order to support his point, he uses personal examples from his own family. Do you think introducing this personal element strengthens or weakens Patrick's argument? Why?

Gay People Should Not Be Allowed to Adopt Children

Robert H. Knight

"[In] a homosexual household, there is a deliberate chance to deny a child—for life—of growing up with a father or mother in the house."

Robert Knight is the director of the Culture and Family Institute at the conservative social values organization Concerned Women for America. The following viewpoint is excerpted from testimony Knight provided to the Virginia legislature in 2005 on a proposed bill that would ban adoption by gay people. Knight argues that gay households are neither stable nor natural and that to deprive children of a mother and father is to deny them their inherent rights. Children crave the attentions of parents of both sexes, Knight states, and families of two fathers or two mothers are not acceptable replacements. In banning gay couples from adoption, the legislature will be protecting the best interests of the children, he says.

AS YOU READ, CONSIDER THE FOLLOWING QUESTIONS:
1. How many married couples are on waiting lists to adopt children, according to the National Council on Adoption?
2. What are the three important relationships that children of gay couples miss out on, according to the author?

Robert H. Knight, "Testimony of Robert H. Knight," Virginia Senate Hearing Regarding HB 2921, February 16, 2005.

Good afternoon.

We're here to talk about what's best for children and how to secure for them the best possible adoptive homes.

Public policy should be guided not by what some adults want but by what's actually best for children. In most debates, homosexual activists argue that they "deserve" to be parents or that they "want" to be parents. Well, that's understandable. There's a universal longing to be a father or a mother, but this doesn't mean everyone is equally qualified.

The activists also assert that this is about "equality," but that's not true. A household that is missing an entire parental sex, that is, missing a mother or a father, is not equal to a married household.

When placing children in foster homes, the state should do everything in its power to provide the best chance for them to have a balanced, happy home life. A lot of these children come out of a troubled background. They need the best situation. This means finding homes with a married mother and father—not a home with two homosexuals, or a home with two heterosexuals who are unwilling to make a lifelong commitment to each other. Even with the nation's high divorce rate, married homes are far more stable on average than any other model.

FAST FACT

In the 2000 census, thirty-three percent of lesbian households and twenty-two percent of gay male households reported at least one child living in the home.

Children Want a Mother and Father

This is not about parenting abilities. There are some wonderful single parents who do their best under tough circumstances. But children in single-mother homes can tell you that they don't crave another mom; they want a father. Kids in single-father homes don't crave another daddy; they want a mom. . . .

States Prohibiting Gays from Adopting

States that prohibit unmarried or same-sex couples from adopting.

States that prohibit gays and lesbians from adopting.

Taken from: Human Rights Campaign, "Adoption and Foster Care Laws," July 2006

In the popular film *Sleepless in Seattle*, a desperate little boy goes on the radio to seek a wife for his single father. He's already got a great dad, played by Tom Hanks. The boy does not want another dad; he wants a mom. Yet, we're told that public policy should be indifferent to that boy's needs. To put it another way, do we really think the boy would not notice if, instead of getting new mom Meg Ryan, he wound up with a guy from *Queer as Folk* as his "second dad?"

It's wrong to place a child in a deliberately motherless or fatherless household, especially when there are married couples waiting to adopt. The National Council on Adoption estimates that between 1 million and 2 million married couples are on waiting lists. They are going to China, Russia and Romania at great expense, seeking children. There is no excuse for placing kids in a motherless or fatherless household or one that isn't even bound by a marital commitment.

Denying Children the Right to Opposite-Sex Parents

Even when a straight, single parent adopts a child, there is at least a chance that a husband or wife will eventually join the parent. But in a homosexual household, there is a deliberate choice to deny a child—for life—of growing up with a father or a mother in the house.

Such a child misses out on viewing, up close, three important relationships: between mothers and fathers, husbands and wives, and men and women, not to mention the special ways in which parents of either sex relate to their sons or daughters.

Who among us could say that our father could be replaced by a lesbian, and this would not have made any difference in our lives? Or that our mother could just as easily have been a male homosexual? Men and women are not interchangeable. Mothers and fathers provide crucial things to children that cannot be duplicated in a same-sex household, regardless of the parenting abilities or good intentions of the adults. Every child deserves a first-class adoption, not to become the object of a politically-driven social experiment. . . .

Making New Homosexuals

Since there is no credible scientific evidence that homosexuality is genetic, it makes sense that kids exposed to parental homosexuality will tend to see it as a viable option. This is tragic, since homosexuality has well-documented health risks, especially for young men, but also for young women.

Various medical journals report drastically higher incidences of sexually transmitted diseases, shortened life spans, domestic violence, alcohol and drug abuse, and psychological problems among homosexuals. San Francisco and New York health authorities are now grappling with a new strain of HIV that is resistant to drug treatments and can result in full-blown AIDS within a year or two instead of the usual 10-year incubation. They're also greatly alarmed by a new strain of chlamydia among young homosexual men that is resisting treatment.

Homosexuality aside, it should be no mystery that children need and want both a mother and a father; it's a self-evident truth. It follows that public policy ought to encourage placement of children in married households.

Children Speak Out

Some children of homosexual parents are beginning to speak out and contradict the idea that it's the same as being raised with a mom and dad. I have heard from several people raised by homosexuals who have told me that they are still dealing, years later, with family dysfunction. One woman poignantly related how she felt when she came out of her

Arkansas state Senator Shawn Womack introduces his bill that would ban gays from adopting children.

bedroom one night and saw her father kiss his male lover on the lips. She said she was physically ill and to this day needs counseling.

Here's a letter we received at [conservative policy group] Concerned Women for America from a woman named Emily:

"Thank you, thank you, thank you for all that you are doing to protect children from being placed in homosexual households. I spent part of my teenage years living with my mother and her female lover. It was a heartbreaking and disturbing experience to say the least. The needs of the children MUST be placed before the desires of adults. Throughout my life, the most well-balanced and successful people I encounter come from healthy, loving, traditional families. I wish I did too!"

In conclusion, let me pose a scenario that, I hope, will put this into perspective. Most of you here are married and have children. If something happened to you and your spouse, would you be comfortable having your son placed in a house with two homosexual men, or a house with two lesbians? How about your daughter being placed with two lesbians, or with two homosexual men?

If those scenarios trouble you as to your own children, why would it be okay for other people's children? The state of Virginia owes all foster children a first-class adoption, nothing less.

Thank you.

Gay People Should Be Permitted to Serve Openly in the Military

" 'Don't ask, don't tell' undermines the very freedom . . . servicemen and women have volunteered to defend."

Martin Meehan

Martin Meehan is a Democratic member of the U.S. House of Representatives from Massachusetts. He served in the House since 1993. In 2006, Meehan introduced the Military Readiness Enhancement Act, which would repeal "don't ask, don't tell" policy for gay service members that was instituted during the Bill Clinton administration. In the following viewpoint, Meehan argues that the policy is outdated, expensive, and discriminatory. Congress should instead implement a policy that allows gay people to serve openly in the military, he writes.

AS YOU READ, CONSIDER THE FOLLOWING QUESTIONS:

1. How many times has "don't ask, don't tell" been challenged in federal courts?
2. According to the *Boston Globe* survey cited in the viewpoint, what percentage of Americans favored allowing openly gay people to serve in the military?

Martin Meehan, "Why We Should Repeal 'Don't Ask, Don't Tell," www.house.gov/meehan, April 27, 2006.

[I]n April 2006] a US District Court judge in Boston ruled that while Congress has the authority to bar gays and lesbians from the military, Congress is also the most appropriate outlet for ending that ban.

Judge George A. O'Toole Jr. found that while Congress made a rational decision when it adopted the "don't ask, don't tell" policy barring gays from serving openly in the military, "deciding that Congress has made a rational choice is not the same as deciding it has made a wise choice." He added that "the remedy for bad decision-making by the political branches is to be found in the working of the political process."

This was the ninth time the "don't ask, don't tell" policy was challenged unsuccessfully in federal court and the strongest statement yet that the way to overturn this outdated and discriminatory policy is

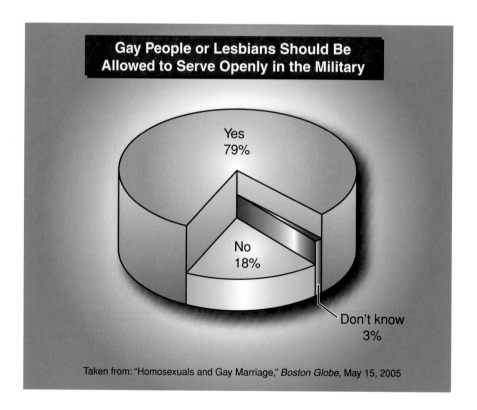

Gay People or Lesbians Should Be Allowed to Serve Openly in the Military

Yes
79%

No
18%

Don't know
3%

Taken from: "Homosexuals and Gay Marriage," *Boston Globe*, May 15, 2005 with legislative, not legal action. Judge O'Toole sent a strong message to the 12 plaintiffs in the case and to Congress that it is time to seriously reconsider the military's "don't ask, don't tell" policy.

Policy Is Outdated

This policy has proven to be unpopular and costly, and there seems to be little convincing evidence for it to remain in effect. In the 12 years since the ban was enacted [in 1993] public opinion has shifted in favor of repealing "don't ask, don't tell." A July 1993 NBC/*Wall Street Journal* poll showed that only 40 percent of people favored allowing openly gay people to serve in the military. But a May 2005 poll conducted for *The Boston Globe* found that 79 percent of people favored allowing openly gay people to serve. It is time for Congress to catch up with the country and overturn this policy.

While public opinion polls show that "don't ask, don't tell" is wildly unpopular, it is also costly to taxpayers in terms of dollars spent to enforce it and costly to our military readiness as we discharge soldiers with skills critical to fighting the wars in Iraq and Afghanistan. [In 2005] the Government Accountability Office released a study showing that the cost of enforcing "don't ask, don't tell" in the first 10 years was more than $190 million. A revised estimate by the University of California at Santa Barbara released in February [2006] found the cost to be almost double the original number—more than $363 million.

The Policy Is Expensive and Wasteful

At a time when our military is already stretched to the breaking point, wasting taxpayer dollars by discharging competent service members under "don't ask, don't tell" doesn't make sense. This money could be better spent protecting soldiers in the line of duty, instead of discharging brave Americans who proudly serve in our military just for being gay. "Don't ask, don't tell" under-

> **FAST FACT**
>
> From 1980 to 1990, about 17,000 service members were discharged from the United States military because they were homosexual. There was no evidence given or required that their behavior had a negative impact on their ability to perform their duties.

mines the very freedom these servicemen and women have volunteered to defend.

With renewed confirmation that overturning "don't ask, don't tell" must happen through legislation, it is in Congress's hands to end this outdated policy and replace it with one of nondiscrimination. [In 2005] I introduced H.R. 1059, the Military Readiness Enhancement Act, which would repeal the military's policy of forced discrimination and replace it with one that would better serve the needs of our armed forces. While this legislation has bipartisan support in Congress and 113 cosponsors, the Republican leadership has refused to even hold a hearing on the bill.

The "don't ask, don't tell" policy is destructive to the principles of our Constitution, the fabric of our communities, and the lives of gay service members and Americans. The United States has proven time and again that we will not stand for policies that endorse discrimination against any group of people. We have proven that we will not tolerate discrimination based on race or gender. Now Congress must make clear that we won't stand for discrimination based on sexual orientation.

EVALUATING THE AUTHOR'S ARGUMENTS:

In the viewpoint you just read, author Martin Meehan argues that the "don't ask, don't tell" policy is both unnecessary—because a majority of Americans favor allowing openly gay people to serve—and discriminatory. Review each of these points in the article. In your opinion, which is the most compelling? Is it more important for Congress to end policies with which most Americans do not agree or policies that discriminate against groups of people?

Gay People Should Not Be Permitted to Serve Openly in the Military

Elaine Donnelly

"Gay activists will not stop pushing their agenda, but the law [barring gays from the military] deserves continued support."

Elaine Donnelly is the president of the Center for Military Readiness, a nonprofit organization that works to discourage the presence of gay people in the military, among other goals. In the following viewpoint, Donnelly references the remarks of General Peter Pace, who says that homosexuality is immoral and akin to adultery. Pace is merely echoing the law passed by Congress in 1993, Donnelly writes, that barred gay people from serving. Moreover, she states, the Bill Clinton administration used different language when it created the "don't ask, don't tell" policy that was meant to enforce the law passed by Congress. The original law needs to be upheld, she writes, and gay people should be barred from military service.

Elaine Donnelly, "General Pace and the PC Police," Center for Military Readiness, www.cmrlink.org, March 26, 2007.

1. According to the author, how did then-president Bill Clinton alter the law passed by Congress that stated "Homosexuality is incompatible with military service?"
2. Using context from the article, define the military term "unprogrammed separations."
3. In the author's opinion, what should Secretary of Defense William Gates do to discourage gay people from joining the military?

Marine Gen. Peter Pace, Chairman of the Joint Chiefs of Staff, should not apologize for supporting the law excluding homosexuals from the military. That law, Section 654, Title 10, was passed with veto-proof bipartisan majorities in both houses of Congress in 1993. Federal courts have declared it constitutional several times.

Nor should Gen. Pace be intimidated by name-calling gay activists who are berating the general for expressing his personal opinions on immorality. A relentless public relations campaign is promoting their cause and a controversial bill [the Military Readiness Enforcement Act], sponsored by Rep. Marty Meehan (D-MA), which would repeal the 1993 homosexual conduct law.

The statute reflects the views of people who see the issue in moral terms, but it uses secular language emphasizing military discipline. Duly enacted laws, including prohibitions against lying, stealing, and murder, should not be repealed just because they coincide with religious principles and moral codes such as the Ten Commandments.

FAST FACT

Although most of America's allies allow gays to serve in the military, many of those countries discourage homosexuals from serving and impose certain restrictions on those who do.

Contradictions in the Law

The personal values of General Pace are not unusual, but two contradictions in his March 12 [2007] statement deserve a closer look. General Pace said that "don't ask, don't tell" allows gay individuals to serve, but that frequently stated misinterpretation lacks support in the law that Congress actually approved.

General Pace also equated homosexuality with adultery, a moral offense that is prohibited under Article 134 of the Uniform Code of Military Justice. Using the general's comment as a teaching moment, consider what would happen if President [Bill] Clinton had imposed on the military a "don't ask, don't tell" policy on adultery. Such a policy could condone adulterous relationships in the military, as long as the people involved do not say they are adulterers. That would encourage illicit behavior, in the same way that the "don't ask, don't tell" policy, imposed by the Clinton Administration, condones dishonesty about homosexual conduct.

Differences Between the Law and the Enforcement Policy

This is why Congress rejected the "don't ask, don't tell" concept in 1993. Instead, members decided to codify pre-Clinton Defense Department regulations stating, *"Homosexuality is incompatible with military service."*

Three months after signing the law—apparently with fingers crossed behind his back—Bill Clinton undermined the statute by announcing contradictory enforcement regulations—the policy known as "don't ask, don't tell." These regulations state that *"sexual orientation"* (a vague phrase appearing nowhere in the law) is *"personal and private"* and *"not a bar to military service."*

The contradiction between the law and Clinton's enforcement policy created confusion that continues to this day. In 1996 the Fourth Circuit Court of Appeals recognized that the "don't ask, don't tell" regulations were inconsistent with statutory language stating, *"The prohibition against homosexual conduct is a longstanding element of military law that continues to be necessary in the unique circumstances of military service."*

Failure to resolve the disparity between policy and law advantages gay activists, because the statute is slandered every time it is mislabeled with the catch phrase "don't ask, don't tell." Chronic confusion helps their high-powered public relations campaign, which frequently cites questionable "studies" and public opinion surveys that are skewed to promote open homosexuality in the military.

Statistics Have Been Misrepresented

In December 2006, for example, Zogby International released a poll that was commissioned by the Center for the Study of Sexual Minorities in the Military, a gay activist group now called the Michael D. Palm Center. The Zogby news release publicized an innocuous question about respondents' relative "comfort" with homosexuals, but omitted mention of the key question displayed on the pollster's website: *"Do you agree or disagree with allowing gays and lesbians to serve openly in the military?"*

On that question, 26% of respondents agreed, but 37% disagreed. The poll also found that 32% of respondents were "Neutral," and 5% were "Not sure." The combined 69% who were opposed or neutral outnumbered the 26% who wanted the law repealed. This was hardly a mandate for radical change.

Another PR [public relations] strategy, shedding crocodile tears about national security, blames the homosexual exclusion law for military personnel shortages. But the often-cited 2005 General Accountability Office [GAO] report, which provided statistical data on the number of "unprogrammed separations" between 1994 and 2003, did not support that claim.

The Pentagon's Office of Personnel and Readiness responded to the GAO report by putting discharge numbers into perspective. During the nine years in question, there were 26,446 discharges for pregnancy; 36,513 for violations of weight standards; 38,178 for "serious offenses;" 20,527 for parenthood, and 59,098 for "drug offenses/use."

In contrast, 9,501 persons were discharged when they acknowledged homosexual conduct—approximately 5 percent of unplanned separations, or 0.37 percent of discharges for all reasons. That number could be reduced to near zero if potential recruits were accurately informed that gay men and women are not eligible to serve in the military.

Homosexuals Should Not Serve

Secretary of Defense William Gates should exercise his legally authorized option to reinstate "the question" about homosexuality that used

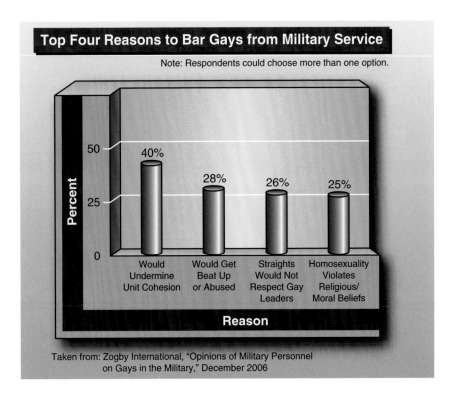

Top Four Reasons to Bar Gays from Military Service

Note: Respondents could choose more than one option.

Taken from: Zogby International, "Opinions of Military Personnel on Gays in the Military," December 2006

to appear on induction forms. At the very least, President [George W.] Bush should drop Clinton's expendable "don't ask, don't tell" regulations, and provide accurate information about the meaning and purpose of the law.

The statute recognizes differences between military and civilian life, and notes that in combat, bonds of personal trust and unit cohesion are essential for mission accomplishment. Such realities justify numerous restrictions on personal behavior that would not be acceptable in civilian life.

Simply stated in gender-neutral terms, the law says that in conditions "characterized by forced intimacy, with little or no privacy," persons should not have to expose themselves to persons who might be sexually attracted to them. The same principle protects privacy between military men and women, to the greatest extent possible. It encourages good order and discipline by respecting the normal human desire for modesty in sexual matters.

Gay activists will not stop pushing their agenda, but the law deserves continued support.

EVALUATING THE AUTHOR'S ARGUMENTS:

In the viewpoint you just read, author Elaine Donnelly compares allowing gay people to serve in the military with allowing those who commit adultery to serve. Both situations, she argues, would encourage dishonesty about behavior. Do you agree or disagree with this comparison? Are homosexuality and adultery similar behaviors? Explain your reasoning.

Chapter 3

Should Gay People Be Permitted to Marry?

The debate over same-sex marriage has led to many protests througout the U.S.

Gay Marriage Should Be Permitted

John Kusch

> "A matter like same-sex marriage, which involves civil rights, religious freedoms, and the sanctity of familial ties, should not be a matter of opinion polls."

In the following viewpoint, John Kusch argues for the legalization of same-sex marriages. He asserts that the definition of marriage has changed a great deal, and the institution of marriage serves different purposes for different individuals, whether financial, spiritual, or emotional. Kusch contends that same-sex marriage can be included in the already broad definition of legal marriage, and that such unions can be recognized by the government without demanding universal support from religious bodies or society. John Kusch is a writer and Internet developer. He keeps an online log, *Letters from a Strip of Dirt,* through which he comments on politics and culture.

John Kusch, testimony before the Wisconsin Joint Legislative Committee, August 21, 2003.

AS YOU READ, CONSIDER THE FOLLOWING QUESTIONS:
  1. Why did the church not allow Kusch's parents to marry?
  2. What does Kusch mean when he explains that marriage "falls under multiple ownership"?
  3. According to Kusch, do supporters of same-sex marriage seek a change in the definition of marriage?

Today, [August 21, 2003] you will likely be presented with an avalanche of figures and statistics on the topic of same-sex marriage, including polls demonstrating what percentage of the public is either in support or opposition, surveys estimating the number of same-sex households in the United States, studies claiming that the percentage of gay and lesbian Americans is ten percent or twenty percent or two percent, and speculative pieces on the potential effects of same-sex marriage on children, homes, religions and society as a whole.[1] As British politician George Canning once said, "I can prove anything by statistics—except the truth."

The truth, it seems to me, is that a matter like same-sex marriage, which involves civil rights, religious freedoms, and the sanctity of familial ties, should not be a matter of opinion polls. Instead of attempting to persuade this committee [Wisconsin Joint Legislative Committee] with facts and figures, I would rather inform the committee by telling the story of an unconventional marriage without which I would not be here today. Of course, I'm speaking of my parents.

Another Story of the Right to Marry

In 1969, my mother was in the difficult position of being a Catholic divorcée with six children to fend for. Even today she would have struggled despite the governmental and community resources available to single mothers, but at the time her situation was truly desperate.

Luckily, my mother met a strong, loving, hardworking man, also a Catholic, who was willing to take her as his wife and take on her six children as his own. The man who would become my father,

---

[1]This was presented as testimony before the Wisconsin Joint Legislative Committee to express opposition to the Assembly Bill 475/Senate Bill 233 "Defense of Marriage Act."

had an unshakeable belief in the importance of family loyalty that I still admire to this day. Such men were and are rare.

Yet despite their obvious love for one another and their willingness to accept both the joys and the responsibilities of family life,

Gay couples believe that they should be allowed to share the same benefits of marriage as straight couples.

my parents were still Catholics, and the Church refused to annul my mother's previous marriage. [This despite the fact that her first husband physically abused her, engaged in flagrant adultery, and inadequately provided for her and her children.] According to Catholic teachings, they were forbidden to marry, as their relationship violated the proscriptions against sex outside marriage. From the Catholic viewpoint at that time, my parents' union was not merely an objectionable marriage: it was a contradiction in terms. It was, simply, not a marriage. Through the lens of the Church, their relationship—their family—was reduced to a sex act.

The irony is not lost on me when today my relationship is compared by certain religious persons to various degrading sex acts.

A Union Outside the Church

Unable to marry in a Catholic ceremony, my parents were instead married before a judge, and the following year, I was born. Despite the Catholic position that my parents were not actually married and

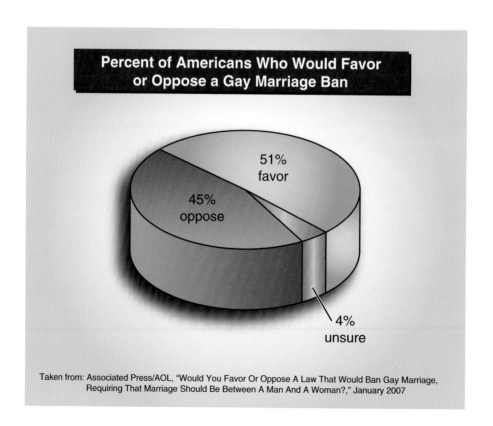

Percent of Americans Who Would Favor or Oppose a Gay Marriage Ban

51% favor

45% oppose

4% unsure

Taken from: Associated Press/AOL, "Would You Favor Or Oppose A Law That Would Ban Gay Marriage, Requiring That Marriage Should Be Between A Man And A Woman?," January 2007

that I was an illegitimate child, I had two loving parents who cared and provided for me, along with my older brothers and sisters. We weren't a family, yet we were a family. As a child, I was understandably confused.

As an adult, I understand that the reason my parents were allowed to marry is that the government rightly understood that despite certain religious objections, my parents had voluntarily entered into a committed familial relationship, forming close bonds of kinship and interdependence, and that as a family it was in their best interest and thus in the interest of the greater community that their union have financial and legal stability that would allow them to support, protect and nurture one another and their children. Furthermore, the government understood that just as my parents were unable to force the Church to bless their union, no individual or group could prevent their union on purely religious grounds. In this way, the government respected the right of religion to define and enforce moral standards among its members while also respecting the right of individuals to adhere to moral standards of their own.

Without this compact of respect between government, religion, and the individual, a marriage like that of my parents—a marriage without which I might not have ended up here before you today—would never have been possible.

To Whom Does Marriage Belong?

It seems to me that the legislation currently under consideration by this committee raises a difficult question: Who owns marriage? In other words, who defines marriage, who allows marriage, and who enforces it? One possible answer is that the government owns it by virtue of its power to enact legislation that grants married persons certain privileges while charging them with certain responsibilities. Another answer is that religions own marriage, as each faith develops certain ceremonies and traditions that seek to define marriage in the context of spiritual life. Yet another answer is that society owns marriage, through its natural tendency to organize itself in ways that help families survive and to enforce those survival strategies through tradition and social pressure.

Yet any one of these answers seems to come up short in the face of such an old and weighty institution. Is marriage a sacrament, a contract, or a social condition? As someone who has had ample opportunity to ponder the meaning of marriage, I am led to believe that marriage not only falls under multiple ownership, but that marriage itself cannot be called a single institution.

Consider for example my parents who, having forgone a religious ceremony, still enjoyed the legal benefits of marriage and were considered a married couple by their peers. Consider also the couple who are joined in a religious ceremony and who function as a married couple in their community, but who for whatever reason do not register their union with the state. And in the case of same-sex marriage, consider the growing number of same-sex couples who consider themselves married, whose extended families and social peers consider them married, whose local governments consider them married, and whose employers consider them married—all despite the fact that according to the state and federal government (as well as several major religions), their marriage is a legal and spiritual impossibility.

Marriage Has Changed Over Time

These examples demonstrate that marriage already enjoys a wide range of definitions and applications, and that ownership of the marriage contract does not and cannot reside in any one governmental, religious, or social body. While it cannot be denied that the concept of same-sex marriage is a new (and for many people revolutionary) concept, proponents of same-sex marriage do not demand a change in the definition of marriage so much as an acknowledgement from the governing bodies that represent them that the definition of marriage has already changed.

It is perfectly understandable that certain groups and individuals, distressed at what they perceive as the erosion of a sacred religious vow, would seek to protect it by using the power of government to prevent further change. Yet to wield the power of government in order to enforce a singular and inflexible definition of marriage would satisfy some at the cost of disenfranchising a significant and growing segment of the population for whom marriage is a very different institution from what it was a decade or a century ago.

Those of us who strive for the legalization of same-sex marriage believe that government can fully represent a broad spectrum of citizens while at the same time respecting the sovereignty of religion and the needs of society. While we assert our right to participate in civic life and to form our own families and our own communities, we understand that our civil liberties do not entitle us to force our way through church doors or to demand societal approval or religious sanction. Those dialogues must be entered into on a local scale—church by church, community by community....

At issue today is the foundation of what we call civil society. Is it possible for the government to respect my choice of mate—in my case, another man—despite the fact that parts of society might disagree with that choice? And if not, is it then appropriate that a distant cousin of mine could qualify as next of kin, whereas my partner of three years could not? My parents contradicted convention and religious teachings in order to give me a safe, stable home life. I am here today to ask each of you to consider that I might deserve a chance to try to be the husband my father was the day he married my mother.

EVALUATING THE AUTHOR'S ARGUMENTS:

In the viewpoint you just read, John Kusch argues that the institution of marriage has already evolved significantly and that all people should have the opportunity to unite a supportive family. In the following viewpoint, Tim Leslie argues that because gay people cannot produce children naturally, they have little reason to marry, as it will not benefit society. With all of the existing changes to marriage that Kusch describes, what might be some of the arguments for preserving the traditional family that Leslie supports?

Viewpoint

2

Gay Marriage Should Not Be Permitted

Tim Leslie

"The spousal union produces families, and such families are the building blocks of society."

In the following viewpoint, author Tim Leslie argues that the heart of marriage is not the spouses' mutual pleasure, but rather the producing and rearing of children. Therefore, society should only support traditional marriage between a man and a woman. He claims that traditional matrimony is the foundation of society and that gay marriage would harm society. In addition, Leslie argues that same-sex couples do not produce a healthy environment in which to raise children, and that gay marriage would lead to a societal breakdown. Tim Leslie is a former California Assemblyman.

AS YOU READ, CONSIDER THE FOLLOWING QUESTIONS:
1. Leslie claims that the happiness of a couple is important, but is not the primary purpose for marriage and never has been. How does he defend this statement?
2. What does Leslie argue is the reason why our society will slide into social chaos if homosexual partnerships are equated with marriage?
3. What does Leslie claim that homosexuals themselves freely admit about marriage?

Tim Leslie, "The Case Against Same-Sex Marriage." www.lifesite.net/ldn/2004/feb/040223a.html, February 23, 2004.

Anyone not living in a cave has noticed the intensifying attack on traditional marriage. In Vermont, Canada, and Massachusetts—and now California, with the signing of a de facto gay marriage bill—the war drums against traditional matrimony are beating with ever-growing intensity.

The onslaught will not be turned back unless the public is given better, more coherent arguments against same-sex spousal unions. While religion plays an obvious role in the debate, the effectiveness of faith-based arguments is limited because most Westerners care little what the Bible or theologians say. To argue from religion will only convince those who are already convinced and will simply alienate the rest.

So how can we assemble a coherent and persuasive case? By steering the discussion back to the historical understanding of marriage's primary end.

In recent generations, we've seen the belief evolve that the overriding purpose of marriage is the spouses' mutual pleasure. This is what enabled Sally Lieber (D-San Jose), my colleague in the California assembly, to say, "I don't see how my marriage is any more moral than the same-sex couples I know." This claim, of course, only makes sense if companionship and sexual pleasure are matrimony's preeminent [greatest] ends.

But this deviates from what every culture in history has recognized as the heart of marriage: the begetting and education of children. The happiness of the couple is vital, to be sure, but it's not the only or primary purpose and never has been. Why? Because "happiness" produces no definitive benefit for society, whereas the rearing of children clearly does. As the Vatican recently noted, "Society owes its continued survival to the family, founded on marriage."

Because of this, it makes sense for society to support traditional marriage alone. Conversely, allowing same-sex spousal unions makes no sense. Indeed, we can only allow homosexual spousal unions if the central purpose of marriage is the spouses' happiness. If that's

Many people believe that marriage should be reserved exclusively for unions between men and women.

true, then heterosexual-only wedlock is indeed discrimination. But if marriage has a higher purpose, then anything that undermines its traditional framework also threatens to undermine its desired result— the rearing of healthy, productive, contributing citizens.

Promoting the General Welfare

If the central purpose of government is to promote the general welfare, then the state must promote always what is best for society's health, security, and long-term viability. This requires the state to make prudential judgments about various segments of our population: Those under 16 may not drive. Those under 21 may not drink. You must possess a high-school diploma to join the military. Information about paroled child molesters must be made available so parents can protect their children.

Some label these prudential decisions "discrimination," but discriminating in such matters promotes the general welfare. The unique affirmation of heterosexual marriage operates under the same principle. Traditional matrimony is the foundation of society, and society should neither encourage nor recognize anything pretending to approximate it. Again, the reason for this relates to marriage's primary purpose: The spousal union produces families, and such families are the building blocks of society.

Granted, many marriages don't produce children. Most soldiers don't face combat and yet are still eligible for veterans' benefits. But the state rewards each institution based on its ability to provide society with a valuable function. Governments favor historical marriage and seek to strengthen it in its policies because virtually everything that happens in society, for good or ill, can be traced back to families and family life.

The Marriage Revolution Would Destroy Matrimony

The marriage revolution would not only undermine matrimony—and thus society—but it would effectively destroy it.

Gay Assemblyman Mark Leno asked during the floor debate for the California gay marriage bill, "Is marriage so fragile?" The answer is yes. The marriage rate is at an all-time low. Fifty percent of marriages end in divorce. Annually, more than one million children experience divorce, and they will suffer in many ways as a result. More couples than ever are living together outside of marriage, which several studies show leads to an even higher divorce rate.

By equating homosexual partnerships with marriage, society's attitudes toward marriage will be cheapened to an even greater degree. As Canadian TV show host Michael Coren notes, "If marriage is suddenly fundamentally altered to include people of the same gender, it loses its genuine meaning to the rest of us. We may include the earthworm in the cat family. Does this make worms feline? Of course not. But it destroys the definition of cat." Instead of being recognized as the crucial, indispensable building block of society—through which most of its benefits flow—marriage will simply be another choice among many. "What's the big deal about marriage?" our children and grandchildren will ask. In the Sixties, this was a fringe sentiment. If gay marriage goes through, it will become the norm.

And as that happens, our society will slide with ever greater speed down the slope of social chaos. Why? Because it will only further encourage marital instability and broken homes, and children growing up in these situations are more likely to exhibit a variety of antisocial behaviors.

Children growing up in traditional homes, on the other hand, have these problems to a significantly diminished degree. They have better emotional health, engage in fewer risky behaviors, are less likely to engage in premarital sex, and do better educationally and economically. Finally, a recent Utah study found that divorce costs the federal, state, and local governments $33 billion per year. For all these reasons, the state has a vested interest in promoting stable traditional marriages.

Furthermore, these marriages provide the natural complementarity between the sexes, which benefits children. Studies show mothers devote special attention to their children's physical and emotional needs, whereas fathers devote their primary efforts to character traits. David Popenoe of Rutgers University's National Marriage Project writes, "Both dimensions are critical for an efficient, balanced, and human child-rearing regime." Left unsaid is the fact that same-sex couples can never provide this complementarity and thus cannot provide an optimally "efficient, balanced, and human child-rearing regime."

Same-Sex Couples Are Fundamentally Different

Still, some would argue, since gays will continue adopting, shouldn't we encourage same-sex marriage? Wouldn't this help give children the stability they need? No, because studies by even homosexual researchers reveal that same-sex couples are fundamentally different from their straight counterparts. They are more promiscuous, have greater physical and mental health problems and shorter life expectancies, and the average duration of relationships is woefully short.

And these differences don't produce a healthy environment in which to raise children. Any number of indicators prove this; indeed, they prove that it would be detrimental and possibly even dangerous. For instance, the journal *Adolescence* reported that researchers found a "disproportionate percentage—29 percent—of the adult children of homosexual parents had been specifically subjected to sexual molestation by that homosexual parent, compared to only 0.6 percent of adult children of heterosexual parents having reported sexual relations with their parent.... Having a homosexual parent(s) appears to increase the risk of incest with a parent by a factor of about 50."

So, while same-sex marriage might promote a particular welfare—that of the couple—it would not promote the general welfare, which arises from raising healthy, balanced children who have all the interior resources necessary to become contributing citizens.

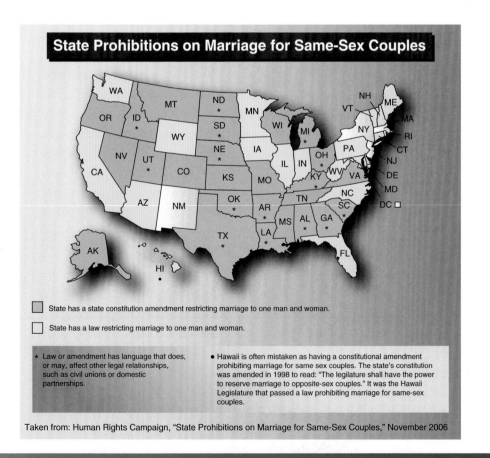

State Prohibitions on Marriage for Same-Sex Couples

☐ State has a state constitution amendment restricting marriage to one man and woman.

☐ State has a law restricting marriage to one man and woman.

* Law or amendment has language that does, or may, affect other legal relationships, such as civil unions or domestic partnerships.

• Hawaii is often mistaken as having a constitutional amendment prohibiting marriage for same sex couples. The state's constitution was amended in 1998 to read: "The legislature shall have the power to reserve marriage to opposite-sex couples." It was the Hawaii Legislature that passed a law prohibiting marriage for same-sex couples.

Taken from: Human Rights Campaign, "State Prohibitions on Marriage for Same-Sex Couples," November 2006

Infidelity and Promiscuity

Gay "marriage" would further redefine marriage in the way it treats conjugal fidelity.

In their book *The Male Couple: How Relationships Develop*, David McWhirter and Andrew Mattison found that of the 156 couples they studied, 75 percent of the partners learned within five years that for the relationship to survive, cheating had to be tolerated, as long as one or the other did not become emotionally involved with the other sex partner. In her book *The Mendola Report*, lesbian Mary Mendola conducted a nationwide survey of approximately 400 homosexual couples. She, too, found that homosexuals distinguish between sexual and emotional exclusivity. Indeed, just 26 percent of homosexuals believe commitment is paramount in a marriage-type relationship.

This translates to an almost unfathomable degree of sleeping around. A recent Amsterdam study found that men in homosexual relationships cheat with an average of eight partners a year. Others have found that the average homosexual has between 100 and 500 sexual partners over his or her lifetime. One study showed that 28 percent have had 1,000 or more sex partners, with another study placing the percentage between 10 and 16 percent.

While adultery is certainly a factor in traditional marriages, it is comparatively rare. In fact, studies on matrimony place the male fidelity rate between 75 and 80 percent and that of females between 85 and 90 percent. The reason is simple: Unlike homosexual relationships, emotional and sexual fidelity within matrimony are inexorably linked and always have been by definition. To extend the concept of marriage to a situation wherein fidelity is not the norm would not only cheapen the institution, but it would have disastrous consequences for children. Simply put, a marriage is not a marriage without total exclusivity.

Homosexuals argue that marriage would make their relationships more stable. However, given the runaway promiscuity in this subculture, the assertion is at best unlikely. As UCLA [University of California Los Angeles] sociologist Anne Peplau notes, "There is clear evidence that gay men are less likely to have sexually exclusive relationships than other people."

Their argument also fails to take into account the institutions that have relaxed prohibitions against homosexuals. The most poignant example of these is the Roman Catholic priesthood. It was argued in the 1960s that allowing gay men into the clerical state would instill in them sexual restraint and celibacy. Just the opposite happened. Most of these men have consciously subverted the historic norms of priestly celibacy. Furthermore, the sex-abuse scandal was largely driven by homosexual priests in that 90 percent of victims were adolescent boys. One study of 50 gay Catholic priests found that only two abstained from sexual activity. Many were very open about their carnal habits. Therefore, we should seriously question the homosexual community's soothing words regarding the consequences of gay marriage.

In response, gay activists point to Vermont and its civil unions and note the sky has not fallen there. However, people said the same thing immediately after the changing of divorce laws, which set in motion forces that would not be evident for 40 years. Says one homosexual researcher who opposes same-sex marriage, "This new experiment would be unprecedented in human history, and yet we haven't taken the time to think carefully about possible consequences. Instead, we've allowed emotion to sweep aside all other considerations."

Goal for Many is to Transform the Notion of "Family"

The final reason same-sex marriage would have a detrimental effect on society comes from homosexuals themselves: Many freely admit they want to redefine marriage, not only to include same-sex couples but to change its very scope and meaning.

Patti Ettelbrick, former legal director of the [gay rights organization] Lambda Legal Defense and Education Fund, once said, "Being queer is more than setting up house, sleeping with a person of the same gender, and seeking state approval for doing so.... Being queer means pushing the parameters of sex and sexuality, and in the process transforming the very fabric of society."

Michelangelo Signorile, homosexual activist and writer, says the goal of homosexuals is to "fight for same-sex marriage and its benefits and then, once granted, redefine the institution of marriage completely, to demand the right to marry not as a way of adhering to society's moral codes but rather to debunk a myth and radically alter an archaic institution.... The most subversive action lesbians and gay men can undertake...is to transform the notion of 'family' entirely."

Even when homosexuals are circumspect about their intentions, their goals are clear. Gay pundit Andrew Sullivan has said the "openness" in many gay relationships would in reality fortify heterosexual marriages by allowing straight couples to see that adultery doesn't necessarily destroy a marriage. Furthermore, once gay "marriage" is allowed, the faithful nature of traditional unions will be transformed accordingly. He says this is a good thing.

None of us should hate those with same-sex attractions. But while embracing them as people made in the image and likeness of God, we should instead make it clear that our problem is with their agenda because it goes against God's plan and would do great damage to our culture and its future stability. These are complex arguments and do not fit easily into a news producer's need for a sound bite. However, we must make the case for the central importance of marriage for society. If we don't, it will result in an unprecedented societal breakdown every bit as catastrophic as the disintegration of the great cultures of the past.

EVALUATING THE AUTHOR'S ARGUMENTS:

In the viewpoint you just read, author Tim Leslie argues that marriage, as a whole, is not about the spouses' mutual pleasure. Marriage is an economic and social arrangement to produce children and thus benefit all of society. Do you agree with this definition of marriage? Why or why not? What do you think is the purpose of marriage? Explain your opinion.

Gay Unions Will Harm the Institution of Marriage

Glenn T. Stanton

"Same-sex proponents are asking everyone—all of society—to dramtically and permanently alter their definition of family."

Glenn T. Stanton is a policy analyst for Focus on the Family, a conservative, Christian-based family values group located in Colorado Springs, Colorado. The following viewpoint argues that permitting gay marriage or same-sex civil unions will erode the institution of marriage. Stanton asserts that the laws of nature, as well as the history of civilization, support heterosexual marriage. Marriage between a man and a woman promotes the public good and provides the healthiest environment for children, he contends.

AS YOU READ, CONSIDER THE FOLLOWING QUESTIONS:

1. How does Stanton contrast objections to same-sex marriage with historical laws against interracial marriage?
2. In Stanton's view, what were the problems with the pronouncement by the American Academy of Pediatrics regarding families with same-sex parents?
3. What is the author's response to what he calls the "Mr. Potato Head" theory of gender?

Glenn T. Stanton, Ten Persuasive Answers to the Question . . . "Why Not Gay Marriage?" Focus on the Family, 2005.

The battle on this issue is at the water cooler and in the church pews. Here are *the* 10 questions relevant to this debate. Master the responses to these questions and you will be well-suited to defend the family.

"How will my same-sex marriage hurt your marriage?"

We're asked this question in nearly every public debate. Our opponent usually brings it up while pointing to his or her partner, whom we meet just before the debate.

If this were *only* about *your* marriage, we say, then maybe we could work something out. If we're only talking about the two of you, then no real harm will be done. But we are not only talking about you two.

Same-sex proponents are asking *everyone*—*all* of society—to dramatically and permanently alter their definition of family, to say that male and female are not essential for marriage, family and society. They want us to believe male and female are merely optional for the family.

Saying male and female don't really matter is harmful to all of us.

No Comparison to Interracial Marriage

"Is same-sex marriage like interracial marriage?"

Same-sex marriage and interracial marriage are nothing alike. Segregation was an evil social problem. Marriage as an exclusively heterosexual union is profound social good. Racism is about power and suppression . . . about keeping the races apart, and that is *wrong.*

Marriage is about bringing male and female together, and that is good.

Marriage has nothing to do with race. It has everything to do with a husband and wife working together to create and care for the next generation.

Striking down bans on interracial marriage affirmed marriage by saying that any woman has a right to marry any man. Same-sex marriage redefines marriage—saying men and women are optional for the family.

And what is more, it is a very different thing for a child to say, "I have a black mother and a white father," than to say, "I have two moms and no father."

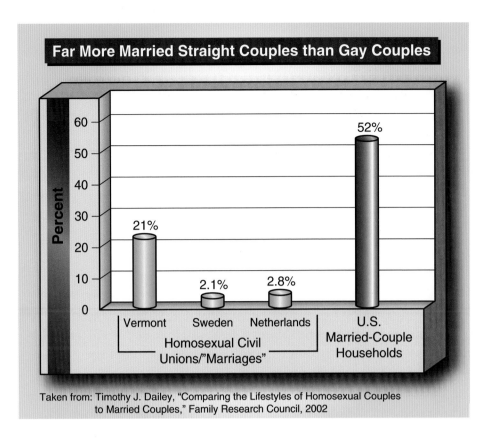

Far More Married Straight Couples than Gay Couples

Taken from: Timothy J. Dailey, "Comparing the Lifestyles of Homosexual Couples to Married Couples," Family Research Council, 2002

There is no research showing interracial parenting is developmentally harmful to children, but literally thousands of studies indicate that children are hindered developmentally when they are denied their mothers or fathers.

What is most troubling about this argument is it implies that people who value the necessary contributions men and women bring to marriage are bigots. This is a vile implication and has no place in civil discourse!

Imposing Limits
"Where does it stop?"

If we say marriage is not about husband and wife, mother and father, where do we stop in our redefinition? Andrew Sullivan, a homosexual writer, says, "The right to marry whomever you wish is a fundamental civil right."

Really?

What would he say to Jonathan Yarbrough and Cody Rogahn?

They were the first couple to get a same-sex marriage license on May 17, 2004, in Provincetown, Mass. When the media asked Yarbrough about their relationship, he said, "I think it's possible to love more than one person and have more than one partner. . . . In our case, it is. We have an open marriage."

What will we tell these men when they want to bring their new love interests into their marriage?

When Cheryl Jacques, former director of the homosexual lobbying group Human Rights Campaign, was asked why same-sex marriage wouldn't lead to multiple-party marriages, she said "Because I don't approve of that."

Wow!

Here's our question for Cheryl: "How come your disapproval of polygamy is more reasonable than my disapproval of same-sex marriage?"

Same-sex marriage is not about tolerance; same-sex homes are tolerated in society. This is about forcing everyone to accept these experimental families.

Here's another question: If same-sex marriage is legalized, could the statement, "Children need a mother and father" be deemed hate speech? It is becoming exactly that in Massachusetts. The *Boston Globe* complained [in 2005], "Governor [Mitt] Romney is denigrating gay families, practicing divisive, mean-spirited politics . . . by insisting that every child 'has a right to a mother and a father.'"

Swedish Pastor Ake Green was threatened with prison for preaching from the Bible about homosexuality.

Only months after same-sex marriage became legal in some parts of Canada, legislators there passed a law that carries a maximum two-year jail sentence for saying certain things about homosexuals. . . .

Don't be surprised, either, when churches are forced to perform same-sex wedding ceremonies.

Does anyone really believe the ACLU will not challenge churches when they refuse to honor their "constitutionally protected" same-sex marriage? In fact, the Catholic Church is being challenged in Canada because a local parish refused to rent out their church reception hall when they learned the reception was for a lesbian couple.

The fact is, once same-sex marriage is legalized, there is no logical stopping point. When you tear marriage away from its moorings, the ship can drift anywhere.

Marriage as a Human Institution

"Can't we all just get along by having religious marriage and civil marriage?"

Some ask, 'Why can't you just keep your religious idea of marriage, and just give us our own kind of civil marriage?"

Well, marriage is more than a religious institution. It shows up in *all* civilizations, not just Christian or religious ones.

Actually, marriage is a human institution that involves both church and state. Churches are interested in making sure marriages are healthy and strong, and city hall—as well as state and federal governments—is interested in what marriage provides society. Maggie Gallagher, a columnist who writes often about marriage, explains:

> There is scarcely a dollar that state and federal government spends on social programs that is not driven in large part by family fragmentation: crime, poverty, drug abuse, teen pregnancy, school failure, mental and physical health problems.

Every society needs men and women to cooperate in founding homes and raising children, and marriage is the way *all* societies accomplish this.

Contributing to a Healthy Society

"What public good does marriage provide?"

Marriage produces and raises the next generation of humanity, which every society needs. If you don't believe this is a need, look at the current depopulation trends in much of Europe. Governments there are realizing that a dearth of childbearing couples raises many serious social and economic issues.

Spin a globe and pick any place on earth and visit that place at any time in human history; you will find that they do marriage one way—*between men and women.* There may be other diversities, such as number of spouses and division of labor, but marriage is *always* heterosexual.

Why do we find this global and historic universality of marriage?

- Is it because Jerry Falwell or Dr. [James] Dobson [Focus on the Family's founder] have gone everywhere, throughout all time, and forced marriage on all cultures?
- Is it a political trick of the Republican Party?
- Did the Catholic Church enforce it on everyone, everywhere?

No.

Nature enforces and imposes marriage upon all human civilizations, and it does so with very little tolerance.

Conversely, there is no public need for the same-sex family. If there were, societies would have created such families to meet the need. But they have not, because same-sex "marriage" meets a personal desire of a few adults, not society as a whole. . . .

A loving and compassionate society comes to the aid of motherless and fatherless children, but no compassionate society *intentionally* subjects children to motherless or fatherless families. *But this is what every same-sex home does—and for no other reason but to satisfy adult desire.* . . .

No society anywhere has been able to sustain itself with a buffet-like mentality of family, where you simply go through the line, pick and choose what suits you and one choice is just as good as another.

Same-Sex Families Are Unfair to Children

"Is it healthy to subject children to experimental families?"

Not all married couples have children, but most do. And not all same-sex married couples will want children, but many of them will. So the argument for same-sex marriage *is* the argument for the same-sex family.

No society at any time—primitive or developed, ancient or modern—has ever raised a generation of children in same-sex homes.

Same-sex marriage will subject a generation of children to the status of lab rats in a vast, untested, social experiment. . . .

Medical Professionals Chime In

"But haven't medical and psychological groups said same-sex parenting is fine?"

We often hear it said that the American Academy of Pediatrics [AAP] supports same-sex parenting. And so does the American Psychological Association [APA], the American Psychiatric Association [APA] and the American Medical Association [AMA].

"Who are you to say they are wrong?" we're asked.

Well, the AAP and APA[s] and AMA *are* wrong. Let's examine why. Here's the American Academy of Pediatrics' statement:

[T]here is a considerable body of professional literature that suggests that children with parents who are homosexual have the same advantages and the same expectations for health, adjustment and development as children whose parents are heterosexual.

Now how did the AAP—all the pediatricians—come to this decision? Did they gather all the best pediatricians together and carefully study the literature, or did they do it another way?

They did it another way.

They made this decision with a select committee of nine people. And once they made this statement, the reaction of the larger membership of the Academy was phenomenal!

Consider this e-mail, written by the lead author of the AAP's study, and what it says about the larger membership's response:

The AAP has received more messages—almost all of them CRITICAL—from members about the recent policy statement on [same-sex adoption] than it has EVER received on any other topic. This is a serious problem, as it means that it will become harder to continue the work that we have been doing to use the AAP as a vehicle for positive change (emphasis in original).

Consider that last statement: ". . . use the AAP as a vehicle for positive change." *Is this careful science or blatant activism?*

Lack of Long-Term Studies

The AAP and these other professional medical organizations cannot make statements about how same-sex families serve the well-being of children.

Why?

Because we have not performed the experiment yet! The AAP admits there are no large populations of children raised in same-sex homes to study:

> The small and non-representational samples studied and the relatively young age of most of the children suggest some reserve. . . . Research exploring the diversity of parental relationships among gay and lesbian parents is just beginning.

Yet within sentences of these recognized cautions, the Academy claims:

> [T]he weight of evidence gathered during several decades using diverse samples and methodologies is persuasive in demonstrating that there is no systematic difference between gay and nongay parents in emotional health, parenting skills, and attitudes toward parenting.

It's also worth noting that while the AAP states the kids who grow up in same-sex homes look pretty much like children who grow up in hetereosexual homes, they are both right and wrong. The fine print of the Academy's study tells the full story. They report that children who grew up in same-sex homes had outcomes similar to children who grew up in heterosexual *divorced* and *stepfamily* homes. That is another way of saying kids who grew up in same-sex homes *didn't* look like kids who grow up with their own mother and father! . . .

Determining What's Best for Children
"How do we know what kind of families children need?"
All of the family experimentation over the past 30 years—no-fault divorce, the sexual revolution, cohabitation and widespread fatherlessness—have been documented failures, harming adults and children in far deeper ways, for longer periods of time, than even the most conservative among us ever imagined.

Why do we think this radical new experiment will somehow bring good things?

No pediatrician or child development theorist would look at a child, see the problems that child has and say, "I know exactly what that

Some of those who oppose same-sex marriages believe that allowing gays to marry would undermine the foundation of our society, the family.

child needs, I'm going to write a prescription for a same-sex home."

Every child-development theory tells us kids do best when they are raised by their own mothers and fathers. And it's interesting that even more liberal organizations are starting to understand this.

Child Trends, in a recent [2002] research brief, explains:

> An extensive body of research tells us that children do best when they grow up with both biological parents. . . . Thus, it is not simply the presence of two parents, as some have assumed, but the presence of *two biological parents* that seems to support children's development.

The Center for Law and Social Policy, also finds:

> Most researchers now agree that together these studies support the notion that, on average, children do best when raised by their two married, biological parents.

By definition, no child living in a two-parent, same-sex home is living with both biological parents. As a result, every child living in such a home is living in a home that is less than best.

Families Should Meet Children's Needs
"Is the same-sex family about the needs of children or the wants of adults?"

We can learn a lot from the world's most famous lesbian mom: Rosie O'Donnell.

In an interview on ABC's "Primetime Live" a few years ago [in 2004], Diane Sawyer asked, "Would it break your heart if he [Rosie's 6-year-old son, Parker] said, 'I want a mommy and a daddy'?"

Rosie said, "No. And he has said that."

Diane said, "He has?"

Rosie answered, "Of course he has. But as I said to my son, Parker, 'If you were to have a daddy, you wouldn't have me as a mommy because I'm the kind of mommy who wants another mommy.'"

Can anyone say that is a good parenting ethic? The child *needs* a daddy, but he is told "no" because the parent has *wants* and those wants come before the child's needs.

Many people say marriage is about legal benefits and privileges—Social Security benefits and hospital visitation rights, and children should be given these benefits and protections. But little Parker has never asked, "Mama, why can't we have all the rights and benefits and protections of marriage?" Parker asks, "Mama, why can't I have a daddy?" And again, the answer is: You can't have what you *need*, because I *want* what *I* want. . . .

Today, we are making unwarranted assumptions about children simply because such assumptions arise from adult wishes. We must realize how this new gigantic social experiment will change the experience of growing up.

The Importance of Gender
"Does gender really matter?"

This is the question this whole issue comes down to. If same-sex families and male-female families are interchangeable—like vanilla or chocolate ice cream, mere preference— and that is exactly what our opponents want us to believe, then. . . .

- male or female

- mother and father
- husband and wife

. . . do not really matter for the family or society. We are told, "You can have a man and a woman in your family if you want, but neither is necessary."

The same-sex marriage proponents take what I call a "Mr. Potato Head" theory of humanity: There is no real difference between Mr. and Mrs. Potato Head. They have the same central core, but merely external interchangeable parts. There's no real difference.

That's exactly what many believe. But no.

Humanity is demonstrated in our complementary beings as male and female.

And male and female *really* mean something.

Our maleness and femaleness go right to the very core of our being. Every person matters as a male or female. Each has what the other needs but lacks.

Love will not be enough to help two dads guide a scared, young girl through her first period or help her pick out her first bra. These men will have very little to say because they've never experienced these things. Likewise, what kind of message would two lesbian moms teach a little girl about loving a man or a little boy about growing into a man?

The same-sex family celebrates sameness.

Any family that intentionally rejects either male or female—saying either is not necessary—cannot be viewed as good and virtuous in a society that esteems the unique value of both male and female.

The idea that male and female are replaceable is really an anti-human message.

EVALUATING THE AUTHOR'S ARGUMENTS:

The author sets up this viewpoint in a question-and-answer format. Do you believe this format would enable opponents of same-sex marriage to more effectively debate this issue? Why or why not?

Gay Unions Will Not Harm the Institution of Marriage

Rosemary Radford Ruether

> "[A]t a time when a third of American households consist in single people, why is it a threat to marriage that homosexual people are embracing marriage?"

In this viewpoint, Rosemary Radford Ruether argues that same-sex marriage is good for the institution of marriage as a whole. So many families today are broken, divorced, or single-parented, and homosexuals' rights to marry would allow for more family units to be stable, committed, and supportive, in the author's view. Ruether contends that gay marriage may even be a positive example for currently unmarried heterosexuals to commit to another person and create successful families. Rosemary Radford Ruether is the Carpenter Emerita Professor of Feminist Theology at Pacific School of Religion. She has written extensively to critique Christian conservatism.

Rosemary Radford Ruether. "Marriage between Homosexuals Is Good for Marriage." *National Catholic Reporter* 42.5 (Nov 18, 2005): 20(1).

AS YOU READ, CONSIDER THE FOLLOWING QUESTIONS:

1. According to Ruether, what reasons do some conservatives give for opposing same-sex marriage?
2. How do Scanzoni and Myers, discussed in the viewpoint, describe the "good way of life"?
3. Why does the author feel that it is illogical to say that homosexual marriage, as opposed to heterosexual marriage, would lead to promiscuity and other questionable patterns?

In the current culture wars, we are constantly told by conservatives that gay marriage would be a disaster for the ideal and institution of (heterosexual) marriage. James Dobson, founder of the conservative evangelical group Focus on the Family, has opined. "Barring a miracle, the family as it has been known for more than five millennia will crumble, presaging the fall of Western civilization itself." Pope John Paul II judged same-sex unions as "degrading" marriage. The Vatican declaration "Considerations Regarding Proposals to Give Legal Recognition to Unions between Homosexual Persons" (2004) stated, "Legal recognition of homosexual unions obscure basic values which belong to the common inheritance of mankind."

But are these warnings that gay marriage poses a threat to marriage true? Do they make either logical or empirical sense? At a time when fewer Americans are marrying at all and many are divorcing, at a time when a third of American households consist in single people, why is it a threat to marriage that homosexual people are embracing marriage? Shouldn't we find the large numbers of people who are unmarried, often raising children as single parents, the prime threat to marriage? What is remarkable about the current movement for marriage among gay people is that they are asking for basically the same institution and ideals of marriage as heterosexuals currently enjoy. They want a publicly recognized sealing of a

FAST FACT

Legal marriage in the United States brings with it over one thousand additional benefits.

Some people feel that allowing gays to marry would strengthen marriage as an institution by holding them accountable for the same standards of marriage as straight couples.

commitment to a lifelong monogamous union with another person with whom they want to share their lives, an institution that also carries with it certain legal rights, such as shared pensions and health plans. Why is this a threat to marriage?

If marriage is not allowed for gay people, what is the alternative that conservative Christians are demanding? For some, gay people shouldn't exist at all; they can and should be converted to heterosexuality. But few medical and psychological experts now share this view. Sexual orientation has proved to be deeply embedded and not easily changed. Another alternative is lifelong celibacy. But celibacy has generally been recognized in the Christian tradition to be a special gift, not given to most people. Why should all gay people be assumed to have this gift? If conservative Christians demand that gays remain unmarried, but they are not capable of celibacy, what are we saying? That they should be promiscuous, that they should have uncommitted relations?

Gay Marriage Is Pro-Marriage

Two evangelical writers, Letha Scanzoni, author of the 1978 book *Is the Homosexual My Neighbor?*, and David Myers, professor of psychology at Hope College in Holland, Mich., have published a book this year arguing for gay marriage from a Christian evangelical perspective, *What God has Joined Together: A Christian Case for Gay Marriage*. In this book they argue that marriage, in the sense of a permanent, life-long, egalitarian, monogamous relationship between two persons for mutual care and child raising, is a fundamental human good. Couples in such relations are healthier and happier. Children are best raised in a stable two-parent household. If this is good for heterosexuals, then it is also good for homosexuals. Gay marriage does not destroy marriage, but rather extends this same good way of life to homosexuals.

The argument that opening marriage to gay people is a slippery slope that will quickly lead to promiscuity, group marriage, polygamy and incest makes no sense. Gay people and heterosexuals have both been promiscuous and pursued various extramarital relations. The gay marriage movement is precisely a rejection of casual and plural

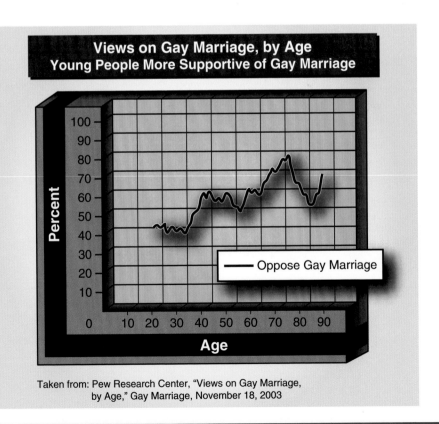

Taken from: Pew Research Center, "Views on Gay Marriage, by Age," Gay Marriage, November 18, 2003

relations. It is an option for a committed, monogamous relationship with one other beloved person for the rest of one's life, One of the remarkable things about the recent opening of marriage to homosexuals, briefly in San Francisco and then in Boston, is the number of gay people who came forward with great joy to seal officially what in many cases had already been a committed relationship of 10, 20 or 30 years. Are gay people "capable" of committed monogamous relationships? Obviously so, at least as much as heterosexuals. What they are asking is for this committed, monogamous relationship to be legally recognized as marriage.

Ms. Scanzoni and Dr. Meyers argue that accepting gay marriage, far from threatening marriage, will confirm and strengthen the ideal of marriage itself for all of us, heterosexuals and homosexuals. Gay marriage can be a positive example for the many people in our society who hesitate and fear to embrace a permanent monogamous and lifelong relationship, with its struggles as well as its joys. Gay marriage should be embraced by Christians as pro-marriage, not anti-marriage. In Ms. Scanzoni and Dr. Meyers' words, "It can prompt heterosexual men and women to appreciate marriage in a new way."

EVALUATING THE AUTHOR'S ARGUMENTS:

In this viewpoint, Ruether presents homosexual unions as pro-marriage, rather than as anti-marriage. Do you agree that same-sex relationships can produce successful families and act as positive examples for marriages of all kinds? If not, can you make sense of the arguments that Ruether claims are illogical?

The Constitution Should Be Amended to Ban Gay Marriage

George W. Bush

"If we are to prevent the meaning of marriage from being changed forever, our nation must enact a constitutional amendment to protect marriage in America."

George W. Bush is the forty-third president of the United States. In 2004, Bush called for an amendment to the federal Constitution that would define marriage as being between a man and a woman, thus banning gay marriage. Congress passed a similar measure in 1996, the Defense of Marriage Act, but localities and states have found loopholes that allow them to marry people of the same sex. In order to uphold the Defense of Marriage Act and defend the basic unit of society, the family, Bush declares, the Constitution must be amended. The following viewpoint is excerpted from a presidential press release.

AS YOU READ, CONSIDER THE FOLLOWING QUESTIONS:

1. What San Francisco event does the president cite as an attempt to redefine marriage?

George W. Bush, "President Calls for Constitutional Amendment Protecting Marriage," Remarks by the President, www.whitehouse.gov, February 24, 2004.

G ood morning. [In 1996] Congress passed, and President [Bill] Clinton signed, the Defense of Marriage Act, which defined marriage for purposes of federal law as the legal union between one man and one woman as husband and wife.

The Act passed the House of Representatives by a vote of 342 to 67, and the Senate by a vote of 85 to 14. Those congressional votes and the passage of similar defensive marriage laws in 38 states express an overwhelming consensus in our country for protecting the institution of marriage

Local Efforts to Allow Gay Marriage

In recent months, however, some activist judges and local officials have made an aggressive attempt to redefine marriage. In Massachusetts, four judges on the highest court have indicated they will order the issuance of marriage licenses to applicants of the same gender in May of [2004]. In San Francisco, city officials have issued thousands of marriage licenses to people of the same gender, contrary to the California family code. That code, which clearly defines marriage as the union of a man and a woman, was approved overwhelmingly by the voters of California. A county in New Mexico has also issued marriage licenses to applicants of the same gender. And unless action is taken, we can expect more arbitrary court decisions, more litigation, more defiance of the law by local officials, all of which adds to uncertainty.

After more than two centuries of American jurisprudence, and millennia of human experience, a few judges and local authorities are presuming to change the most fundamental institution of civilization. Their actions have created confusion on an issue that requires clarity.

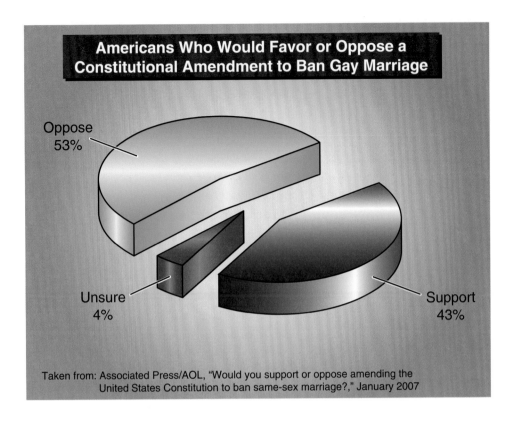

Americans Who Would Favor or Oppose a Constitutional Amendment to Ban Gay Marriage

Oppose
53%

Unsure
4%

Support
43%

Taken from: Associated Press/AOL, "Would you support or oppose amending the United States Constitution to ban same-sex marriage?," January 2007

The Constitution Must Be Amended

On a matter of such importance, the voice of the people must be heard. Activist courts have left the people with one recourse. If we are to prevent the meaning of marriage from being changed forever, our nation must enact a constitutional amendment to protect marriage in America. Decisive and democratic action is needed, because attempts to redefine marriage in a single state or city could have serious consequences throughout the country.

The Constitution says that full faith and credit shall be given in each state to the public acts and records and judicial proceedings of every other state. Those who want to change the meaning of marriage will claim that this provision requires all states and cities to recognize same-sex marriages performed anywhere in America. Congress attempted to address this problem in the Defense of Marriage Act, by declaring that no state must accept another state's definition of marriage. My administration will vigorously defend this act of Congress.

Yet there is no assurance that the Defense of Marriage Act will not, itself, be struck down by activist courts. In that event, every state would be forced to recognize any relationship that judges in Boston or officials in San Francisco choose to call a marriage. Furthermore, even if the Defense of Marriage Act is upheld, the law does not protect marriage within any state or city.

Upholding the Defense of Marriage Act

For all these reasons, the Defense of Marriage requires a constitutional amendment. An amendment to the Constitution is never to be undertaken lightly. The amendment process has addressed many serious matters of national concern. And the preservation of marriage rises to this level of national importance. The union of a man and woman is the most enduring human institution, honoring—honored and encouraged in all cultures and by every religious faith. Ages of experience have taught humanity that the commitment of a husband and wife to love and to serve one another promotes the welfare of children and the stability of society.

Supporters of a gay marriage ban discuss their views on the proposed Marriage Affirmation and Protection Amendment.

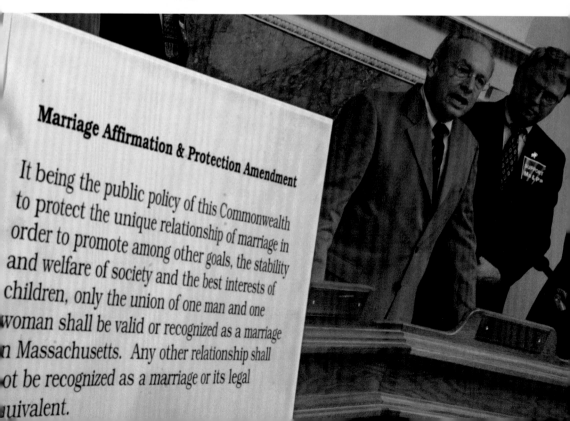

Marriage cannot be severed from its cultural, religious and natural roots without weakening the good influence of society. Government, by recognizing and protecting marriage, serves the interests of all. Today I call upon the Congress to promptly pass, and to send to the states for ratification, an amendment to our Constitution defining and protecting marriage as a union of man and woman as husband

and wife. The amendment should fully protect marriage, while leaving the state legislatures free to make their own choices in defining legal arrangements other than marriage.

America is a free society, which limits the role of government in the lives of our citizens. This commitment of freedom, however, does not require the redefinition of one of our most basic social institutions. Our government should respect every person, and protect the institution of marriage. There is no contradiction between these responsibilities. We should also conduct this difficult debate in a manner worthy of our country, without bitterness or anger.

In all that lies ahead, let us match strong convictions with kindness and goodwill and decency.

Thank you very much.

EVALUATING THE AUTHOR'S ARGUMENTS:

President George W. Bush uses the phrase "protecting marriage" in his argument for a Constitutional amendment. Adam Goodheart, the author of the next viewpoint you will read uses the phrase "banning gay marriage," when referring to the same amendment. How does each author's choice of words influence how you view his argument?

The Constitution Should Not Be Amended to Ban Gay Marriage

Adam Goodheart

"Bush proposed an amendment that would . . . block the possibility for American institutions to keep pace with the times on the . . . subject of homosexuality."

Adam Goodheart is a fellow at Washington College's C.V. Starr Center for the Study of the American Experience, and a regular contributor to *USA Today*, from which this viewpoint was excerpted. Goodheart argues that amending the Constitution to ban gay marriage would be both hasty and damaging to American society. In forcing a vote on the amendment, people would have to choose between two sides, eliminating compromise or alternatives, Goodheart writes. Marriage is the most serious of issues, and any decision of the magnitude of an amendment should be debated carefully.

Adam Goodheart, "Constitutional Amendment Corners Many Americans," *USA Today,* March 1, 2004.

AS YOU READ, CONSIDER THE FOLLOWING QUESTIONS:
1. Identify the two radical camps that George W. Bush's proposal would create, according to Goodheart.
2. To which two other historical instances does the author refer in the viewpoint?
3. What is the "stark choice" Goodheart states that Bush is asking Americans to make?

The president [George W. Bush], speaking on national TV from the White House, has declared me and millions of other law-abiding American citizens unconstitutional. Or so it felt as President Bush urged the nation to pass a constitutional amendment banning gay marriages.

I knew [the February 2004] announcement would come, yet actually hearing it filled me with waves of sadness, shame—and anger.

Like many other gay and lesbian Americans, I believe that marriage—that most private and fundamental of contracts between two people—is a basic human right, one too long denied to us. Like many, I also recognize the breadth of public opinion, from wholehearted support for giving gays the right to marry to passionate opposition. But vast numbers of Americans favor a compromise such as civil unions or simply haven't yet given this suddenly prominent issue much thought.

People Being Forced to Choose

What Bush proposed effectively would force these millions of moderates to choose between two radical camps. He declared gays' desire for equality not just wrong, but so dangerous that we must amend the Constitution to prevent it from being realized, now or ever.

FAST FACT

The Constitution has only been amended sixteen times in the two hundred years since the Bill of Rights was passed.

Most Americans, I believe, would rather ponder this issue for a while, see how things play out in Massachusetts and California [where same-sex marriage amendments were being considered in 2004], then reach their own conclusions. In a sense, they agree with the Founding Fathers, who recognized that as the nation grew and evolved, Americans gradually would develop new ideas about freedom.

Amendment Would Block Evolution of Rights

In 1816, Thomas Jefferson predicted future generations would extend liberty's ideals into realms not yet imagined: "Laws and institutions must go hand in hand with the progress of the human mind," he wrote. "As that becomes more developed, more enlightened, as new discoveries are made, new truths disclosed, and manners and opinions change with the change of circumstances, institutions must advance also, and keep pace with the times."

Speaking from a house once occupied by Jefferson, Bush proposed an amendment that would all but block the possibility for American institutions to keep pace with the times on the rapidly evolving subject

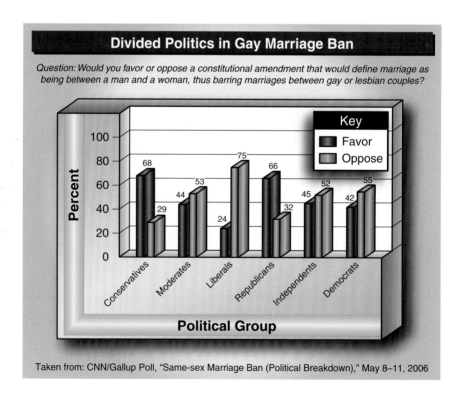

Divided Politics in Gay Marriage Ban

Question: Would you favor or oppose a constitutional amendment that would define marriage as being between a man and a woman, thus barring marriages between gay or lesbian couples?

Taken from: CNN/Gallup Poll, "Same-sex Marriage Ban (Political Breakdown)," May 8–11, 2006

Many of those who oppose an amendment banning gay marriage believe that it is wrong to deny homosexuals what they consider to be a basic human right.

of homosexuality. Indeed, it was one of the rare occasions in history when our government has tried to turn back the clock on freedom and use the Constitution against a specific class of people, as the U.S. Supreme Court did in the 1857 Dred Scott decision, or as President Franklin Roosevelt did when he ordered the internment of Japanese-Americans during World War II.

For me, the president's conclusion was the most insulting part of the entire speech: "In all that lies ahead, let us match strong convictions with kindness and goodwill and decency."

Hey, it's not personal, Bush seemed to be trying to say.

Despite that disclaimer, the fight will be a very personal struggle indeed. The question of gay marriage touches on many people's most closely held private beliefs—not just about love, sex and family, but about religion, fairness and basic notions of right and wrong.

Forcing a Choice on Many

Millions of Americans' views on this are dictated by their feelings for a gay brother, sister, child or close friend. Many are tugged in two directions at once: A heterosexual's religious background might encourage him to condemn same-sex marriage, yet he might also feel sympathy toward a homosexual couple he knows.

Bush is asking these Americans to make a stark choice that many are not prepared to face. Many, even those far from ready to enthusiastically support gay rights, have a "live-and-let-live" attitude. They now are compelled to make choices—religious beliefs vs. family loyalties, for instance—that most don't want to face.

As politicians and ordinary citizens decide which side of the fence they stand on, they will face rancorous discord—not just on the public stage, but also within families and communities. Bush and his allies have created a new issue potentially as disruptive as the abortion question has been for the past three decades. The leader who promised us four years ago that he would be "a uniter, not a divider" has brought this to pass.

EVALUATING THE AUTHORS' ARGUMENTS:

In the viewpoint you just read, Adam Goodheart quotes Thomas Jefferson, one of the nation's Founding Fathers, as saying "Laws and institutions must go hand in hand with the progress of the human mind." From the rest of Jefferson's quotation in the article and from your own knowledge, do you think that Jefferson would agree or disagree with the proposed Constitutional amendment? Why or why not?

Glossary

civil union: a legal act in which a couple is recognized and sanctioned by a civil authority. A civil union usually carries with it some but not all of the benefits and rights of marriage.

Defense of Marriage Act: a 1993 law that gives states and the federal government permission to refuse to recognize same-sex marriage, even if those marriages were legally performed in another state. The law was passed by Congress and signed by President Bill Clinton.

Federal Marriage Amendment: a proposed amendment to the federal Constitution that would define marriage in the United States as only between one man and one woman, thus banning all forms of same-sex marriage. The amendment was proposed by President George W. Bush but failed to pass the Senate in a 2006 vote.

gay: a non-insulting slang word that usually refers to a homosexual man, but can also refer to a homosexual woman.

homophobia: prejudice against or fear of gay men and lesbians.

homosexual: a man or woman who is attracted to members of the same sex.

Lawrence v. Texas: a 2003 Supreme Court case in which state sodomy laws, including those relating to gay men, were ruled unconstitutional and an invasion of sexual privacy. The decision eliminated all remaining state sodomy laws in the United States.

lesbian: a woman who is attracted to other women; a homosexual woman.

pedophile: an adult who is sexually attracted to young children.

sexual orientation: a person's natural preference for sexual partners. Sexual orientation can refer to heterosexuality, homosexuality, or bisexuality.

sodomy: anal or oral sex between a man and a woman or members of the same sex. The word is also used pejoratively to mean any sexual act that is considered unnatural.

Facts About Homosexuality

Same-Sex Relationships in Global History and Culture
- Romances between adult men and boys were considered the norm in ancient Greece and were frequently an important part of the teacher-student relationship.
- Same-sex relationships have been documented in the literature and art of premodern Africa, India, and Arabia.
- Many Native American tribes considered homosexual people to be possessed of "two spirits," and were revered for what was thought to be their increased powers. They were frequently shamans.
- In Iran, Yemen, and Saudi Arabia, homosexual acts are punishable by death. In other Middle Eastern and some African countries, homosexuality is cause for martial punishment or imprisonment.

Homosexuality in the United States
- The American Psychiatric Association (APA) removed homosexuality from the list of mental illnesses in the Diagnostic and Statistical Manual of Mental Disorders in 1973.
- In 1980, a gay high school student in Rhode Island sued his school and won the right to take his boyfriend to prom in the case of *Aaron Fricke vs. Richard B. Lynch*.
- In 2003, the United States Supreme Court ruled that sodomy laws are unconstitutional in the case *Lawrence vs. Texas*. Since then, there are no U.S. states with laws banning sodomy.
- The U.S. military's policy of "don't ask, don't tell" was instituted in 1993 by President Bill Clinton.
- A Harris Interactive poll taken in February 2007 reported that 55 percent of Americans surveyed believed that openly gay people should be able to serve in the military versus 18 percent who said they should not serve at all.
- Black women in lesbian relationships in the United States earn less income and are less likely to own their own home than black women in heterosexual relationships, according to the National Gay and Lesbian Task Force.

Gay Marriage and Unions

- As of 2007, Massachusetts was the only state in the nation to recognize same-sex marriage.
- Connecticut, New Jersey, California, Maine, Vermont, and Hawaii have some form of civil union that offers rights and legal recognition to gay couples, though not marriage.
- The Defense of Marriage Act, which gave the federal government the right to refuse to recognize same-sex marriage, was passed by Congress and signed by President Clinton in 1996.
- In 2001, the Netherlands became the first country in the world to legalize same-sex marriage.
- As of 2007, Belgium, Canada, South Africa, and Spain all recognized same-sex marriage.
- Denmark recognized the world's first same-sex civil union in 1989.
- Same-sex civil unions are legal in over a dozen countries, including France, Spain, Denmark, Finland, Iceland, Israel, and Norway.
- According to the European polling company Eurobarometer, 44 percent of citizens in European Union nations believe that same-sex marriage should be permitted, and 32 percent believe gays and lesbians should be allowed to adopt children.

Homosexuality in the Polls

According to a November 2006 Human Rights Campaign report:

- The number of same-sex couples in the United States has increased by 30 percent since 2001.
- The largest increase occurred in the Midwestern states, including Wisconsin, Minnesota, Nebraska, and Kansas.
- States with the largest total percentage of same-sex couples include New Hampshire, Washington, Massachusetts, and Maine.

According to a poll conducted by Zogby International in 2006:

- 50 percent of respondents believed that sexual orientation is genetic, while 34 percent believed it is partly genetic and partly by choice, and only 11 percent believed it was a conscious choice.
- 47 percent agreed that all people have the potential to be attracted to both sexes, and 62 percent believed that gay people may occasionally be attracted to straight people.

According to a May 2005 Gallup poll:

- 44 percent of Americans surveyed said they believed homosexual relations were acceptable.

Organizations to Contact

The editors have compiled the following list of organizations concerned with the issues debated in this book. The descriptions are derived from materials provided by the organizations. All have publications or information available for interested readers. The list was compiled on the date of publication of the present volume; the information provided here may change. Be aware that many organizations take several weeks or longer to respond to inquiries, so allow as much time as possible.

American Civil Liberties Union (ACLU)
132 W. Forty-third St., New York, NY 10036
(212) 944-9800 • fax: (212) 359-52900
Web site: www.aclu.org
The ACLU is the nation's oldest and largest civil liberties organization. Its Lesbian and Gay Rights/AIDS Project handles litigation, public policy work, and education on behalf of gays and lesbians. The ACLU publishes the handbook *The Rights of Lesbians and Gay Men,* as well as the monthly newsletter *Civil Liberties Alert.*

Canadian Lesbian and Gay Archives (CLGA)
Box 639, Station A, Toronto, ON M5W 1G2 Canada
(416) 777-2755
e-mail: queeries@clga.ca • Web site: www.clga.ca
The CLGA collects and maintains information and material relating to the gay rights movement in Canada and elsewhere. Its collection of records and other materials documenting the stories of lesbians and gay men is available to the public. It also publishes an annual newsletter, *Lesbian and Gay Archivist.*

Children of Lesbians and Gays Everywhere (COLAGE)

3543 Eighteenth St., Suite l, San Francisco, CA 94110
(415) 861-5437 • fax: (415) 255-8345
e-mail: colage@colage.org • Web site: www.colage.org
COLAGE is a national and international organization that supports young people with gay or lesbian parents. Their mission is to foster the growth of children with gay parents by providing education, support and community. Their publications include the newsletter *COLAGE Summary.*

Concerned Women for America (CWA)

1015 15th St. NW, Suite 1100, Washington, DC 20005
(202) 488-7000 • fax: (202) 488-0806
Web site: www.cwfa.org
CWA's purpose is to preserve, protect, and promote traditional Judeo-Christian values through education, legislative action, and other activities. It opposes homosexual relationships and gay marriage. CWA publishes the monthly *Family Voice*, which periodically addresses issues such as homosexuality and gay unions.

Courage

210 W. Thirty-first St., New York, NY 10001
(212) 268-1010 • fax: (212) 268-7150
e-mail: nycourage@aol.com • Web site: http://couragerc.net
Courage is a network of spiritual support groups for gay and lesbian Catholics who wish to lead celibate lives in accordance with Roman Catholic teachings on homosexuality. It publishes listings of local groups, as well as a newsletter.

Equal Rights Marriage Fund (ERMF)

2001 M. St. NW, Washington, DC, 20036
(202) 822-6546 • fax: (202) 466-3540
The ERMF is dedicated to the legalization of gay and lesbian marriage and serves as a national clearinghouse for information on same-sex marriage. The organization publishes brochures and articles, including *Gay Marriage: A Civil Right.*

Family Research Council (FRC)

801 G St. NW, Washington, DC 20001
(202) 393-2100 • fax: (202) 393-2134
Web site: www.frc.org

The council seeks to promote and protect the interests of the traditional family, which it defines as a union between a man and a woman. FRC opposes gay marriage and adoption rights. It publishes numerous conservative position papers on issues affecting the family, including homosexuality, as well as the monthly newsletter *Washington Watch*.

Focus on the Family

8605 Explorer Dr., Colorado Springs, CO 80920
(800) 232-6459 • fax: (719) 531-3424
Web site: www.family.org

Focus on the Family is a Christian organization dedicated to preserving and strengthening the traditional family. It opposes homosexual practice as a rule and takes the stance that homosexuality is a sin. Focus on the Family supports laws to ban gay marriage and adoptions. The group publishes the monthly magazine *Focus on the Family*, as well as the report *Setting the Record Straight: What Research Really Says About the Social Consequences of Homosexuality*.

Human Rights Campaign (HRC)

919 Eighteenth St. NW, Suite 800, Washington, DC 20006
(800) 777-4723 • fax: (202) 347-5323
Web site: www.hrc.org

The HRC provides information on national political issues affecting lesbian, gay, and bisexual Americans. It offers resources to educate congressional leaders and the public on issues such as ending workplace discrimination, combating hate crimes, and fighting HIV/AIDS. The group publishes the *HRC Quarterly*.

Lambda Legal Defense and Education Fund, Inc.

120 Wall St., Suite 1500, New York, NY 10005
(212) 809-8585 • fax: (212) 809-0055
Web site: www.lambdalegal.org

Lambda Legal is a public-interest law firm committed to achieving full recognition of the civil rights of lesbians and gays. The firm addresses a variety of areas, including equal marriage rights, gays in the military, and same-sex parenting. It publishes the quarterly *Lambda Update* and the pamphlet *Freedom to Marry*.

National Gay and Lesbian Task Force

1325 Massachusetts Ave. NW, Suite 600, Washington, DC 20005
(202) 393-5177 • fax: (202) 393-2241
e-mail: theTaskForce@theTaskForce.org
Web site: www.thetaskforce.org
The National Gay and Lesbian Task Force is a civil rights advocacy group that lobbies Congress and the White House on a range of civil rights and AIDS issues. The organization is working to make same-sex marriage legal. It publishes numerous papers and pamphlets, as well as the booklet *To Have and to Hold: Organizing for Our Right to Marry*.

Traditional Values Coalition

139 C. St. SE, Washington, DC 20003
(202) 547-8570 • fax: (202) 546-6403
e-mail: mail@traditionalvalues.org
Web site: www.traditionalvalues.org
The coalition strives to restore what the group believes are traditional moral and spiritual values in American government, schools, and media. It believes homosexuality threatens the family unit and is in general opposition to gay rights. The coalition publishes the quarterly newsletter *Traditional Values Report*, as well as numerous information papers.

For Further Reading

Books

Robert Aldrich, ed., *Gay Life and Culture: A World History.* New York: Universe, 2006. Essays on gay culture from Sumeria to the present.

George Chauncy, *Why Marriage? This History Shaping Today's Debate Over Gay Equality.* Cambridge, MA: Basic, 2005. A history of the gay rights movement in America.

Donald H. Clark, *Loving Someone Gay.* Berkeley, CA: Celestial Arts, 2005. A general reference guide to issues affecting the gay community, including political, moral, and legal events.

Louis Crompton, *Homosexuality and Civilization.* Cambridge, MA: Belknap, 2006. A chronicle of the history of homosexuality in Europe and Asia from ancient times until the eighteenth century.

Timothy Dailey, *Dark Obsession: The Tragedy and Threat of the Homosexual Lifestyle.* Nashville, TN: B&H Publishing Group, 2003. Discusses homosexuality from a biblical and theological perspective.

Ronnie W. Floyd, *The Gay Agenda: It's Dividing the Family, the Church, and a Nation.* Green Forest, AR: New Leaf, 2004. A religious argument against homosexual relationships.

William N. Eskridge and Darren R. Spedale, *Gay Marriage: For Better or for Worse?* New York: Oxford University Press, 2006. The history and ramifications of same-sex marriage in Scandinavia and the lessons for the United States.

Abigail Garner, *Families Like Mine: Children of Gay Parents Tell It Like It Is.* New York: Harper, 2005. A pro-gay book that features interviews with adult children of gay and lesbian couples.

Evan Gerstmann, *Same-Sex Marriage and the Constitution.* New York: Cambridge University Press, 2004. Explores the legal and constitutional effects of the gay marriage debate.

Davina Kotulski, *Why You Should Give a Damn About Gay Marriage.* Los Angeles: Advocate, 2004. This pro-gay marriage book focuses on the rights and benefits extended to married couples.

Erwin Lutzer, *The Truth About Same-Sex Marriage.* Chicago: Moody, 2004. This book, written by an anti-gay-marriage activist, offers a Christian-based view of the issue.

Gerald P. Mallon, *Gay Men Choosing Parenthood.* New York: Columbia University Press, 2004. Offers various portraits and personal stories of gay fathers.

Eric Marcus, *Is It a Choice? Answers to the Most Frequently Asked Questions About Gay and Lesbian People.* San Francisco: Harper San Francisco, 2005. A pro-gay primer that answers general questions about gays and lesbians.

David Moats, *Civil Wars: The Battle for Gay Marriage.* New York: Harcourt, 2004. The history of the U.S. struggle over gay marriage, beginning in 2000.

Daniel R. Pinello, *Gay Rights and American Law.* New York: Cambridge University Press, 2003. A survey of judicial decisions relating to gay rights and an analysis of the thought process behind those decisions.

Alan Sears and Craig Osten, *The Homosexual Agenda: Exposing the Principal Threat to Religious Freedom Today.* Nashville, TN: Broadman and Holman, 2003. This antigay book argues that gay people are undermining the goals of others in America.

Louis P. Sheldon, *The Agenda: The Homosexual Plan to Change America.* Charleston, SC: Frontline, 2005. This antigay book argues that gays and lesbians are attacking the traditional values structure of the nation.

Peter Sprigg, *Outrage: How Gay Activists and Liberal Judges Are Trashing Democracy to Redefine Marriage.* Washington, DC: Regnery, 2004. Argues that traditional marriage needs to be defended from liberal courts.

Glenn T. Stanton and Bill Maier, *Marriage on Trial: The Case Against Same-Sex Marriage and Parenting.* Downers Grove, IL: Intervarsity Press, 2004. Argues that gay people should not be married and are not fit to raise children.

Suzanna Danuta Walters, *All the Rage: The Story of Gay Visibility in America.* Chicago: University of Chicago Press, 2003. An overview of gay culture and politics in mainstream America.

Periodicals

Neela Banerjee, "Gay and Evangelical, Seeking Paths of Acceptance," *New York Times,* December 12, 2006.

Dennis Belkofer, "My Dirty Little Former Secret," *Christianity Today,* April 2006.

Ginia Bellafante, "In the Heartland and Out of the Closet," *New York Times,* December 12, 2006.

Sarah Blackstock, "All Moms Deserve Respect," *Toronto Star,* May 12, 2006.

Bruce Bower, "Gay Males' Sibling Link," *Science News,* July 1, 2006.

Columbus Dispatch, "Prohibiting Parenthood," February 22, 2006.

John Corvino, "Nature? Nurture? It Doesn't Matter," *Between the Lines,* August 12, 2004.

Eric Deggans, "Are They? Who Cares?" *St. Petersburg (Florida) Times,* February 6, 2005.

Economist, "New Fuel for the Culture Wars," February 28, 2004.

Robert Epstein, "Do Gays Have a Choice?," *Scientific American Mind,* February/March 2006.

Ellen Goodman, "Kid Stuff," *Pittsburgh Post-Gazette,* August 9, 2006.

Brad A. Greenberg, "Wrongful Love," *Christianity Today,* September 2006.

Harvard Mental Health Letter, "Who Is Homosexual and the Difference It Makes," December 2006.

Charles C. Haynes, "A Moral Battleground, A Civil Discourse," *USA Today,* March 20, 2006.

Stan Heck, "Gays and the Vatican," *Commonweal,* January 13, 2006.

Jeff Jacoby, "Kids Take Back Seat to Gay Agenda," *Boston Globe,* March 15, 2006.

William Stacy Johnson, "Jesus, the Bible, and Homosexuality," *Theology Today,* October 2006.

Fred Kuhr, "Blind Dateline," *Advocate,* June 21, 2005.

Stanley Kurtz, "End of Marriage as We Know It," *San Francisco Chronicle,* February 29, 2004.

Martin Meehan, "Why We Should Repeal 'Don't Ask, Don't Tell,'" *Boston Globe,* April 27, 2006.

Abram Morgan, "No More Secrets," *Buffalo News*, August 27, 2006.

National Review, "And Now New Jersey," November 20, 2006.

Margaret Cloyd Nelson, "On the Road: Young Gay Activists," *Newsweek*, April 3, 2006.

New Republic, "Down State," March 15, 2004.

David Luc Nguyen, "My Life Away From Exodus," *Advocate*, August 15, 2006.

Stephen Ornes, "Do Brothers Make You Gay?" *Discover*, September 2006.

Vincent P. Pellegrino, "Gays' Late Adolescence," *Newsday*, September 24, 2006.

Christopher Rice, "Monogamy and Me," *Advocate*, February 29, 2005.

Debra Rosenberg, "A Renewed War Over 'Don't Ask, Don't Tell,'" *Newsweek*, November 27, 2006.

Mark Schoofs, "In Nigeria, a Bill to Punish Gays Divides a Family," *Wall Street Journal*, January 12, 1007.

Barry Jay Seltser, "Episcopalian Crisis," *Commonweal*, May 19, 2006.

Bruce C. Steele, "No Special Rights," *Advocate*, January 20, 2004.

Steve Swayne, "The Case for Federal Civil Unions," *Valley News*, February 28, 2004.

Stuart Taylor Jr., "Gay Marriage and the Estate Tax," *National Journal*, July 10, 2006.

Paul Varnell, "Sex, Drugs, Drink and Excuses," *Chicago Free Press*, March 16, 2005.

Shawn Zeller, "A 'Gotcha' Gay Crusade," *CQ Weekly*, July 10, 2006.

Web Sites

Gay and Lesbian Alliance Against Defamation (www.glaad.org). This nonprofit organization is dedicated to promoting positive images of gays and lesbians in the media to combat homophobia. The Web site includes a list of shows that include gay characters and video clips relating to gay issues, as well as a section for gay people of color.

Independent Gay Forum (www.indegayforum.org). The Independent Gay Forum is an online community of gay activists, writers, attorneys, and academics who publish essays and articles on issues currently affecting the gay community. The Web site also includes a blog, CultureWatch.

NoGayMarriage.com (www.nogaymarriage.com). A project of the American Family Association, a conservative social policy group, this Web site centers around an anti-gay- marriage petition to be sent to members of Congress. Visitors to the site can sign the petition as well as information on what the group calls the Marriage Protection Amendment.

SpeakOut.com (www.speakout.com/activism/gayrights). SpeakOut is an online group dedicated to general activism on popular issues. The site includes an extensive section on gay rights, where visitors can sign pro-gay petitions, participate in polls and surveys, and send messages to elected officials.

United Families International (www.unitedfamilies.org). United Families is a group dedicated to preserving the traditional family unit, which it defines as one man married to one woman, along with their children. The group opposes gay unions, including gay marriage, as well as adoption or parenting by gay people. The Web site includes links to other antigay organizations, as well as information on the gay community.

Index

Picture Credits

Cover: © Corbis
Justin Sullivan/Getty Images, 14, 25, 127
David McNew/Getty Images, 18, 86, 111
AP Images, 30, 51, 55, 67, 73, 89, 96, 122
Steve Liss/Time & Life Pictures/Getty Images, 35
Alex Wong/Getty Images, 42, 49
Porter Gifford/Getty Images, 62
Stephen Chernin/Getty Images, 116